Busy Ant Maths

2nd EDITION

Pupil Book 6C

T0340484

Series Editor: Peter Clarke

Authors: Elizabeth Jurgensen, Jeanette Mumford, Sandra Roberts, Linda Glithro

Contents

Mental addition and subtraction

Perform mental calculations including those with large numbers

Challenge 1

1 Work out these calculations mentally.

a
186,430 + 40,000

b
271,538 – 4,200

c
372,300 – 600

d
521,642 + 300,000

e
762,518 + 7,000

f
487,286 – 11,000

g
629,360 + 800

h
400,763 – 12,000

i
840,229 – 500,000

j
377,224 + 8,500

2 Adding or subtracting a multiple of 10, 100 or 1,000 is not difficult. What types of addition and subtraction calculations do you find difficult to calculate mentally and need to use a formal written method for? Include in your explanation some examples of these types of calculations.

Challenges 2,3

1 Work out these calculations mentally.

a   2,670,000

i   + 500,000

ii   + 7,000

iii   – 34,000

iv   – 300,000

b   4,350,800

i   + 54,000

ii   + 6,000

iii   – 400,000

iv   – 3,000

c   5,714,000

i   + 700,000

ii   + 8,000

iii   – 5,000

iv   – 400

d	3,157,800	e	7,000,000	f	4,390,822

d
i + 900
ii + 63,000
iii − 38,000
iv − 400,000

e
i + 175,000
ii + 38,000
iii − 23,000
iv − 300

f
i + 500
ii + 600,000
iii − 56,000
iv − 700,000

2 Play these two games with a partner.

More than 1,000,000

- Both write down the number 10,000. This is your start number.
- Take turns to spin the spinner and roll the dice.
- Each time, put the two together to make a number. So, if you roll a 2 and spin '10,000s', then your number would be 20,000.
- Add your number to the start number.
- Continue until one player's number is greater than 1,000,000. This player is the winner.

Less than 10,000

- Begin with a start number of 1,000,000.
- Play the game as described above, but this time subtract the number you make using the dice and the spinner.
- The winner is the first player whose number is less than 10,000.

You will need:
- Resource 78: Place value spinner
- pencil and paper clip – for the spinner
- 1–6 dice

Develop a different version of the games in Challenges 2, 3 that involves addition and subtraction.

- What will the target number be?
- What will the start number be?
- What kind of dice will you use?
- Will you want a different type of spinner?

I am going to include an unlucky number. If you roll it you miss a turn!

Missing numbers

- Add and subtract whole numbers and decimals using the formal written methods of columnar addition and subtraction
- Estimate and check the answer to a calculation

1 Use rounding to estimate the unknown number in each calculation. Then work out the unknown number.

Example

$465,489 +$ ⬚ $= 749,473$

$\rightarrow 750,000 - 470,000 = 280,000$

```
  6  14  8  13  16  1
  7  4  9  4  7  3
- 4  6  5  4  8  9
  2  8  3  9  8  4
```

a
```
    487273
 +
    829570
```

b
```
    328446
 +
    515228
```

c
```
    732237
 +
    916829
```

d
```
    236472
 +
    851543
```

e
```
    825656
 +
   1556983
```

f
```
    543864
 -
    328547
```

g
```
    473965
 -
    256462
```

h
```
    726834
 -
    408519
```

i
```
    943829
 -
    429316
```

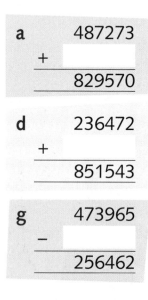

2 Explain how you worked out the unknown numbers in Question 1.

1 Use rounding to estimate the unknown number in each calculation. Then work out the unknown number.

a
```
    5683145
 +
    7995927
```

b
```
    4293562
 +
    6836296
```

c
```
 +  4382175
    9547969
```

d
```
 +  7372145
   10853817
```

e
```
    5287931
 -
    2636461
```

f
```
    7862975
 -
    4447492
```

g
```
    8428715
 -
    2709084
```

h
```
 -  2653425
    3719226
```

i
```
 -  2315463
    6112192
```

2 Use rounding to estimate the unknown decimal in each calculation. Then work out the unknown decimal.

a
```
     56781·23
+          ·
  _____
     83938·16
```

b
```
     48765·41
+          ·
  _____
     84677·80
```

c
```
           ·
+    59232·81
  _____
     91389·03
```

d
```
     87241·34
−          ·
  _____
     61630·82
```

e
```
     94781·59
−          ·
  _____
     41328·38
```

f
```
           ·
−    44256·82
  _____
     31272·94
```

Challenge 3

1 Find three different answers for each calculation.

a
```
  6 2 1 7 8 5 9
+
  _____
      9     3   4
```

b
```
  4 0 8 7 2 9 4
+
  _____
      6       2 1
```

c
```
  5 4 8 6 7 2 1
+
  _____
      9     6     9
```

d
```
  8 4 3 1 5 7 6
−
  _____
      3     2     7
```

e
```
  5 2 9 4 7 6 0
−
  _____
    1 3     5
```

f
```
  6 7 8 1 4 2 5
−
  _____
      4     3     6
```

2 Check your answers to Question 1 with a partner. Do you have any of the same missing digits?

3 Work out where the missing puzzle pieces go in this addition calculation. Some pieces have been put in for you.

Hint

There are multiple solutions to this problem. See if you can find more than one.

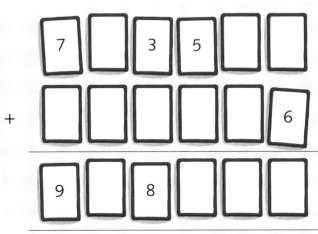

Order of operations (2)

- Use knowledge of the order of operations to carry out calculations involving the four operations
- Estimate and check the answer to a calculation

For each calculation, estimate the answer before you work it out. Then compare your actual answer with your estimate to check your working.

Challenge 1

1 Use the BODMAS rule to work out the answers to these calculations.

a $45 + 16 \times 2$ b $25 + 32 \div 4$

c $40 - 30 \div 5$ d $32 - (5 + 7)$

e $22 \div (15 - 4)$ f $30 \times (8 + 12)$

> **Rule**
>
> The order of operations is:
> **B**   **B**rackets
> **O**   **O**rders (e.g. 4^2)
> **DM**   **D**ivision and **M**ultiplication
> **AS**   **A**ddition and **S**ubtraction
> The way to remember this is:
> **BODMAS**

2 Work out each pair of calculations to see the effect of using brackets.

a $(14 - 3) + 2$

$14 - (3 + 2)$

b $(4 + 8) \times 5$

$4 + (8 \times 5)$

c $(25 - 4) \times 6$

$25 - (4 \times 6)$

d $(24 + 16) \div 8$

$24 + (16 \div 8)$

e $(75 - 15) \div 5$

$75 - (15 \div 5)$

f $(36 \div 6) + 3$

$36 \div (6 + 3)$

Challenge 2

1 Use the BODMAS rule to work out the answers to these calculations.

a $297 \div 9 \times 3 + 450$ b $22 \times (3 + 5) - 42$ c $302 + (48 - 23) \times 5$

d $250 + 3 \times (8 + 4)$ e $350 - (57 + 23) \div 10$ f $23 \times 6 - (123 - 94)$

g $95 \div 5 - (99 - 83)$ h $909 - (823 - 21) + 99$ i $285 \div 3 - (98 - 23)$

j $62 + 15 \times 5 \div 3$ k $856 - (232 + 68) \div 10$ l $200 - (36 + 27) \times 2$

2 Using the numbers and the operations below, with either one or two sets of brackets, make ten calculations. Each calculation must have a different answer and use three operations.

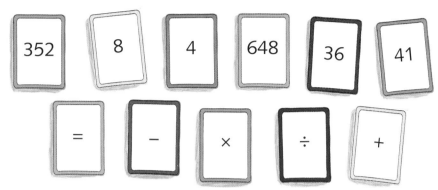

1 Use brackets to make two different answers for each calculation: the smallest possible answer and the largest possible answer.

Example

58 + 60 ÷ 10 − 4
smallest answer: (58 + 60) ÷ 10 − 4 = 7·8
largest answer: 58 + 60 ÷ (10 − 4) = 68

a 422 − 239 + 52 − 50   **b** 25 + 30 × 2 + 38

c 64 + 25 × 15 − 7   **d** 216 − 9 × 8 − 5

e 112 + 56 ÷ 7 + 14   **f** 95 + 190 ÷ 10 + 9

g 243 + 27 ÷ 9 − 3   **h** 936 − 429 ÷ 13 − 2

i 51 × 9 − 6 + 53   **j** 35 × 6 − 18 + 2

k 840 ÷ 5 + 3 × 25   **l** 53 × 3 + 42 − 98

m 144 ÷ 8 × 4 + 16

Hint

Remember, brackets can go round more than two numbers and one operation.

2 Write five calculations, each with three operations, where the answer is the same no matter where you put the brackets. Explain why this is.

Marco's Cafés

- Solve problems involving addition, subtraction, multiplication and division
- Estimate and check the answer to a calculation

For each of these these word problems about Marco's Cafés, use rounding or the inverse operation(s) to check your answers.

1 In December, Marco's customers each paid an extra 5p for a cup of coffee. This additional charge was donated to a local charity. If Marco sold 3,765 cups of coffee, how much did the charity receive?

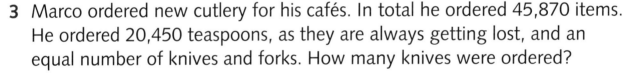

2 The café's speciality is fresh donuts. They are very popular! In November: Café P sold 5,472, Café Q sold double this number, and Café R sold 4,928. What were the total sales?

3 Marco ordered new cutlery for his cafés. In total he ordered 45,870 items. He ordered 20,450 teaspoons, as they are always getting lost, and an equal number of knives and forks. How many knives were ordered?

4 Marco wants new tables for his cafés. The number he needs can be:
- divided by 3 with a remainder of 1
- divided by 5 with a remainder of 3
- divided by 6 with a remainder of 4.

He needs between 50 and 60 tables. How many tables does he need?

1 Marco orders his annual stock of napkins for all three of his cafés at the same time. Café R needs more napkins than Café Q, but not as many as Café P. One café needs 48,680 napkins and another café needs 5,240 more. In total he orders 154,340 napkins. How many does he need to deliver to each café?

2 Marco checked the number of customers who have visited all three cafés. The total for February was 2,311. In March the figure was five times as many. April was also a very busy month. The number of customers for all three months was 28,756. How many visited the cafés each month?

3 Every December Marco's customers pay an extra 3p for each mince pie they buy. This additional charge is donated to charity. Last year, £125.40 was raised. This year an extra 20% was raised. How many mince pies were sold this year and last year?

4 In January, Marco was very surprised when he looked at the donut sales in each café. He noticed that they were three consecutive numbers. The total sales were 13,665. What were the sales for each café?

5 Marco pays his junior staff £8 an hour. In three weeks one junior employee earned £888. Each week he worked 6 hours more than the week before. How many hours did he work each week?

Challenge 3

1 For August, September and October, Marco decided to order cups and paper towels and share them equally between all three of his cafés. The combined total of cups and paper towels he ordered was 25,890. He ordered 3,942 more paper towels than cups.

   a How many paper towels will each café receive?

   b How many cups will each café receive?

2 In June, Marco's customers each pay an extra 5p for every cup of tea they buy. This additional charge is donated to charity. The three cafés together raised £347.60.

   a How many cups of tea were sold?

   b Café P raised 10% more than Café Q. Café R raised £81.95. How much did Cafés P and Q each raise?

Formulae and number sequences

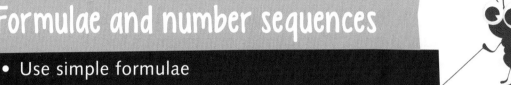

- Use simple formulae
- Generate and describe linear number sequences

1 Simplify expressions **a** to **d** and multiply the brackets in expressions **e** to **h**.

a $3a + 4a + a$ **b** $4x + 3y - y + 2x$

c $5m - 3n + m - 2n$ **d** $5s + 5t - 3t + 3s$

e $2(a + b)$ **f** $5(2x - y)$

g $3(m + 3n)$ **h** $4(2s - 3t)$

2 Calculate the next five numbers in these sequences and explain the rule.

a 6, 10, 14, 18, , , , ,   **b** 80, 72, 64, 56, , , , ,

1 Simplify these expressions by grouping like terms and multiplying the brackets.

a $4(a + 4a + b - 3b)$ **b** $2(2x + 3y - y + 4x)$ **c** $3(m + 2n + 2m - 4n)$

d $3(2s + 4t - t + 2s)$ **e** $5(3m + 4n - 2m - n)$ **f** $4(3x - 2y - 2x + 3y)$

2 Look at these problems and decide which of the equations gives the correct solution. There may be one or two correct solutions.

a Sam had 23 coins in his pocket and used some to buy an ice-cream. He had 11 coins left in his pocket. How many did he use?

$11x = 23$ $11 + x = 23$ $23 + 11 = x$ $23 - x = 11$

b Steve bought a number of pizzas and cut each one into 8 pieces. He had 56 pieces. How many pizzas did he buy?

$p = 56 - 8$ $8p = 56$ $56p = 8$ $p = 56 \times 8$

c The school netball team played 8 matches against other schools and scored 32 goals. What is the equation to show the average number of goals scored?

$g = 8 \div 32$ $\qquad$ $g = 32 \div 8$

$8g = 32$ $\qquad$ $32g = 8$

d A rower trains on his rowing machine by rowing 15 km every day except Sunday. How far does he row each week?

$d = 15 \times 7$ $\qquad$ $d = 15 + 6$

$d = 15 \div 6$ $\qquad$ $d = 15 \times 6$

3 The nth term in a sequence is $2n - 4$. Calculate the first five terms, the 10th term and the 200th term.

4 The nth term in a sequence is $3n + 7$. Calculate the first five terms, the 10th term and the 200th term.

1 Simplify these expressions by multiplying the brackets and grouping like terms.

a $2(3x + y) + 3(2y - x)$ $\qquad$ **b** $6(3a - 2a) + 8(2b - b)$

c $3(2x - y) + 2(x + 3y)$ $\qquad$ **d** $4(2a + 2b) + 2(3a - 3b)$

e $4(t + 5s) + 3(2t - 4s)$ $\qquad$ **f** $5(2a + 2b - a - b) + 4(b - a)$

2 Calculate the next five numbers in these sequences. Work out the nth term and calculate a value for the 100th term and the 250th term.

a 6, 10, 14, , , , , $\qquad$ n^{th} term $\qquad$ 100th term $\qquad$ 250th term

b 3, 10, 17, , , , , $\qquad$ n^{th} term $\qquad$ 100th term $\qquad$ 250th term

Algebra problems

- Express missing number problems algebraically
- Use simple formulae

 Challenge 1

Four boys are throwing javelins.

- Tom threw a javelin x metres.
- John threw a javelin half as far as Tom.
- Jim threw a javelin 12 metres further than John.
- Jack's throw was 3 metres less than Tom.

a Write expressions using x for how far John, Jim and Jack threw their javelins.

b If $x = 50\,m$, calculate how far each of the four boys threw the javelin.

 Challenge 2

1 Find the value of x.

a $3x = 2x + 3$ **b** $2x - 4 = x + 3$ **c** $2 + 3x = x + 4$ **d** $6x - 20 = 10 + x$

2 Three families visit a Theme Park. 'c' is the cost of admission for a child and 'a' is the cost of admission to the Theme Park for an adult. Write an expression for the entry cost for each family.

a Andrews family   **b** Barnes family   **c** Singh family

3 If the cost for a child is £12 and the cost for an adult is £21, calculate the cost for each family and then for your own family.

4 These are the five Platonic solids. They are very special because every face is a regular polygon of the same size and shape: that's why we use them as dice.

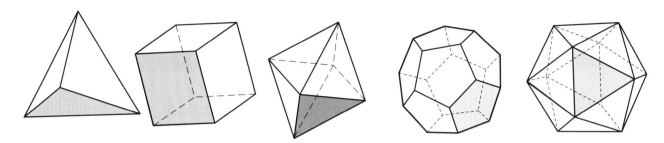

a Draw a table showing the number of faces (F), vertices (V) and edges (E) for the five Platonic solids. Add an extra column for 'F + V'.

b Use the information from the table to write an equation relating F, V and E.

c Do the triangular prism and hexagonal pyramid shown below fit the formula? Choose two more 3-D shapes and see if they fit the formula.

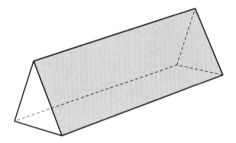
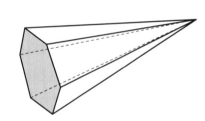

Challenge 3

There are three commonly used temperature scales:

• In Britain, the Celsius scale (°C) is generally used.

• In America, the Fahrenheit scale (°F) is generally used.

• Scientists all over the world use the Kelvin scale (K).

Copy the table below and use the formulas in the Rule box to fill in the missing temperatures.

°Fahrenheit	°Celsius	Kelvin
	0°	
140°		
	37°	
212°		

Rule

• To convert from °Fahrenheit to °Celsius: $C = \frac{5}{9}(F - 32)$

• To convert from °Celsius to °Fahrenheit: $F = \frac{9}{5}C + 32$

• To convert from °Celsius to Kelvin: $K = C + 273$

Linear equations

- Find pairs of numbers that satisfy an equation with two unknowns
- Use simple formulae

1 Here are some sets of coordinate pairs. Complete the rules.

You will need:
- 1 cm squared graph paper
- ruler

Example

(1, 3); (2, 4); (4, 6); (7, 9)   The rule is $y = x + 2$

a (2, 5); (4, 7); (5, 8); (6, 9)   The rule is $y = x +$

b (2, 7); (3, 8); (4, 9); (6, 11)   The rule is $y = x +$

c (4, 3); (7; 6); (9, 8); (10, 9)   The rule is $y = x \ldots$

2 Use your answers from Question 1 and follow the steps below.

- Draw axes on your graph paper and label the x- and y-axes from 0 to 12.
- Plot the points from Question 1 and carefully join the coordinates to show lines **a**, **b** and **c**. Label each line.
- Write what you notice about the lines.

3 There is more than one whole number solution for each of these equations. Find two pairs of numbers that satisfy each equation.

a $2x + y = 8$ **b** $a + 3b = 10$

1 Draw axes on your 1 cm squared graph paper and label the x- and y-axes from 0 to 15.

- Copy the table and complete the values for y.
- Plot the points and carefully join the coordinates to show the three lines. Label each line.
- Write what you notice about the lines.
- Can you draw another line that follows the same pattern? Write down the equation for your line.

	1st set of coordinates		2nd set of coordinates		3rd set of coordinates	
	x	y	x	y	x	y
$y = x + 1$	1		3		7	
$y = x + 4$	2		5		8	
$y = x + 7$	0		2		6	

2 There is more than one whole number solution for each of these equations. Find two pairs of numbers that satisfy each equation.

a $a + 2b = 12$ **b** $x + 3y = 12$ **c** $2a + 3b = 16$ **d** $5x + 2y = 24$

3 Conversion graphs are commonly used to change units from one to another. Use the rules to draw separate conversion graphs for:

a litres to pints **b** kilograms to pounds

> **Rules**
> - $4.5\ l = 8$ pints
> - 5 kg $= 11$ lb

> **Hint**
> You need two points to draw a line. One point can be (0, 0).

4 Use your graphs from Question 3 to calculate an approximate value for:

a 6 pints in litres **b** 3 kg in pounds

c 7 litres in pints **d** 15 pounds in kg

hallenge 3

Draw axes on your 1 cm squared graph paper and label the x- and y-axes from −10 to +10 to create a 4-quadrant coordinates grid.

a Plot the line $y = x − 3$. Find values for y when $x = −5$, 2 and 6 to give you three sets of coordinates.

b Write the coordinates for the points where the line crosses the x- and y-axes.

c Now plot the line $y = x + 3$. Find values for y when $x = −6, −2$ and 4.

d Write the coordinates for the points where the line crosses the x- and y-axes. What do you notice about the two lines?

e Predict where the lines $y = x − 6$ and $y = x + 6$ will cross the x- and y-axes.

f Find three sets of coordinates for each of the lines and plot the lines to check your prediction.

Alternative solutions

- List possible combinations of variables
- Use simple formulae

Hint

Try to be systematic – perhaps using a table to record your results.

Challenge 1

There are 12 legs in the farmyard.

Write an equation to show the possible combinations of chickens and sheep.

Use *c* for the number of chickens and *s* for the number of sheep.

List the solutions for *c* and *s*.

Challenge 2

1 There are 28 legs in the farmyard.

Write an equation to show the possible combinations of ducks and goats.

Use *d* for the number of ducks and *g* for the number of goats.

List the solutions for *d* and *g*.

2 Here are some addition algebra 'brick wall' problems. The numbers in two bricks that are side by side are added together and make the answer in the brick above.

a How many different solutions can you find for *a* and *b* if *a* and *b* are positive integers?

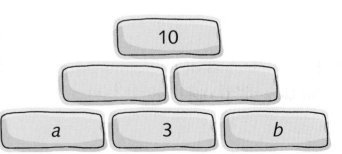

b How many different solutions can you find if x and y are positive integers?

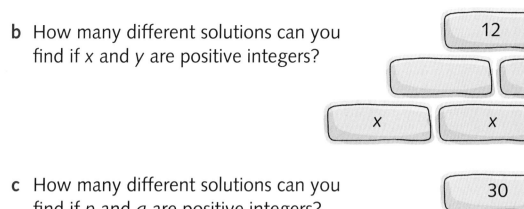

c How many different solutions can you find if p and q are positive integers?

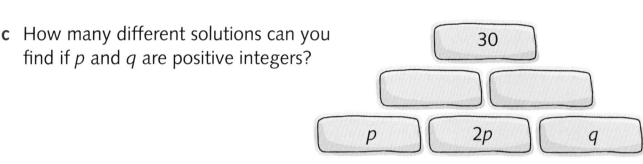

d How can you be sure that you have found all the possible answers?

Challenge 3

1 There are 10 legs in the farmyard. Write an equation to show the possible combinations of chickens, ducks, sheep and goats. Use c for the number of chickens, d for the number of ducks, s for the number of sheep and g for the number of goats. List the solutions for c, d, s and g.

2 Here are some subtraction algebra 'brick wall' problems. The difference between the two numbers in adjacent bricks is calculated to make the answer in the brick above. Work with a partner to find three different solutions to each problem.

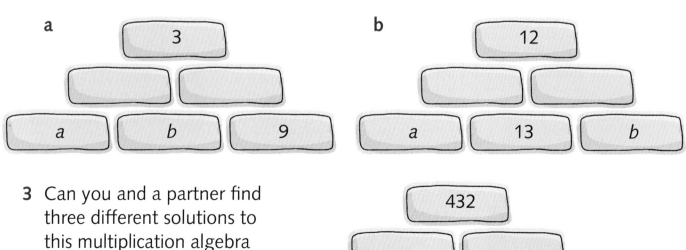

3 Can you and a partner find three different solutions to this multiplication algebra 'brick wall' problem?

Drawing and naming circles

Draw and name parts of circles and know that the diameter is twice the radius

You will need:
- three paper circles
- glue
- ruler

Challenges 1,2,3

Fold each paper circle in half. Then fold it in half again. Stick the circles into your exercise book or on to a piece of paper. Use your fold marks to mark and label each circle as shown below.

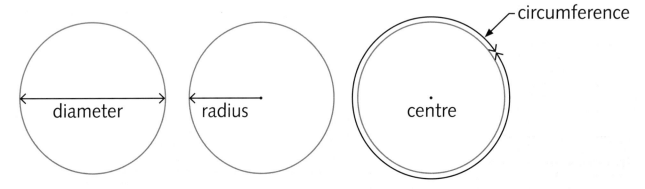

diameter   radius   centre   circumference

Challenge 2

1 Copy this table. Measure the diameter and the radius of each circle below and complete your table.

You will need:
- compasses
- ruler

Circle	A	B	C	D	E
Diameter (cm)					
Radius (cm)					

A

B

C

D

E

2 Using the rule, $d = 2r$, calculate the diameter of each circle. The circles are not drawn to scale.

A
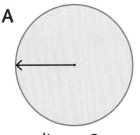
radius = 2 cm

B
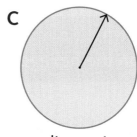
radius = 6 cm

C
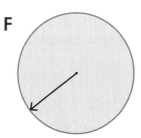
radius = 4 cm

Example

$r = 4.5\,cm$
$d = 2 \times 4.5\,cm$
$\quad = 9\,cm$

D
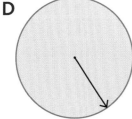
radius = 2·5 cm

E
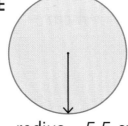
radius = 5·5 cm

F
radius = 3·5 cm

3 Draw the circles in Question 2 and measure their diameters to check your calculations.

4 Using the rule, $d = 2r$, calculate the radius of each circle. The circles are not drawn to scale.

Example

$d = 9\ cm$
$r = 9\ cm \div 2$
$\quad = 4.5\ cm$

A
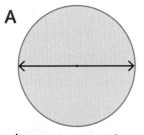
diameter = 12 cm

B
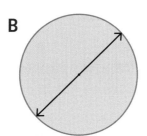
diameter = 15 cm

C
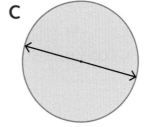
diameter = 19 cm

Challenge 3

Using the reverse side of the 1 cm squared paper and your ruler, draw eight squares with sides of 4 cm, as shown below. Set your compasses to a radius of 2 cm. Make an accurate drawing of the border pattern.

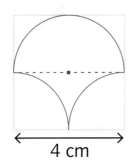
4 cm

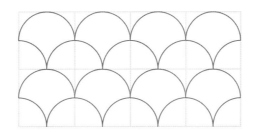

You will need:
• 1 cm squared paper
• ruler
• compasses

Circle patterns (1)

Use compasses to construct a regular hexagon and patterns based on the hexagon

1 Construct a regular hexagon using compasses.

Step 1 Set your compasses to a radius of 4 cm and draw a circle.

Step 2 With your compasses still set to a radius of 4 cm, go round the circumference of the circle, making marks 4 cm apart.

Step 3 Use your ruler to join the points where the marks cross the circle.

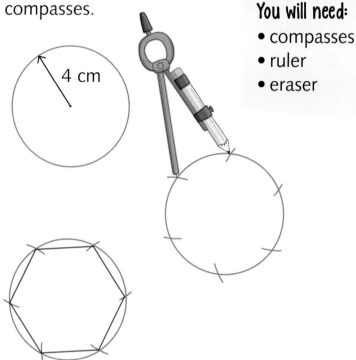

You will need:
- compasses
- ruler
- eraser

2 Using your ruler, construct six equilateral triangles within the hexagon.

1 Construct a basic hexagonal pattern using compasses.

- Follow Steps 1 and 2 in Question 1 of the Challenge above.
- Using one of the marks on the circumference as the centre, draw an arc to cut the circumference twice.
- Repeat five times more, using each mark on the circumference in turn.

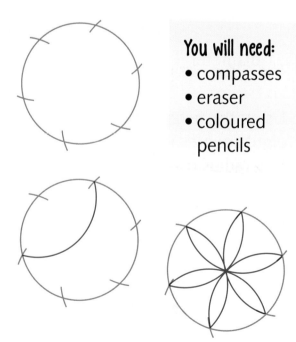

You will need:
- compasses
- eraser
- coloured pencils

2 The three designs below are based on the hexagonal pattern.
Set your compasses to a radius of 3 cm. Draw each design.
Erase the unwanted lines and colour the pattern.

3 Design a hexagonal pattern of your own.

Challenge 3

PQRS is a square with sides of
6 cm. Each vertex P, Q, R and
S is the centre of a circle which
has a radius of 4·2 cm.

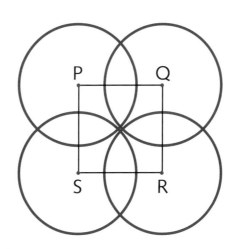

You will need:
• compasses
• protractor
• ruler
• eraser
• coloured pencils

The three designs below have been constructed using the measurements
in the square pattern above. Work out how each design has been made.
Choose two designs to construct and colour.

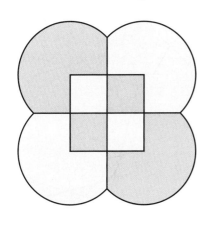  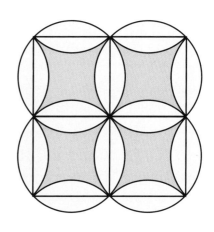

Circle patterns (2)

Use compasses to construct patterns that are based on the radius of a circle

You will need:
- card
- scissors
- ruler
- compasses
- coloured pencils

Challenge 1   Follow the instructions below to construct the pattern.

- Cut out a square of card with sides of 6 cm. Use your ruler to draw one of the diagonals of the square.

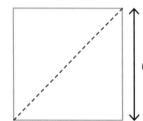

6 cm

- Draw a circle with a radius of 4·2 cm in your book or on a different piece of paper. Make six marks on the circumference with your compasses set at 4·2 cm.

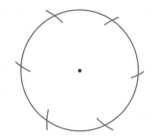

- Join the opposite marks on the circumference to make three diagonals.

- Place the square over the circle. Line up the diagonal of the square with a diagonal of the circle. Draw around the square in pencil.

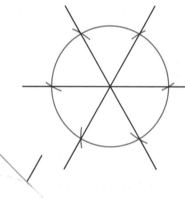

- Turn the square until it lines up with the next diagonal of the circle. Draw round the square. Repeat once more. Then colour your pattern.

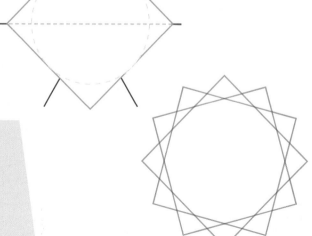

1 Draw a circle with a radius of 5 cm and construct the basic hexagonal pattern. Draw all the lines in this diagram lightly because some will be erased later.

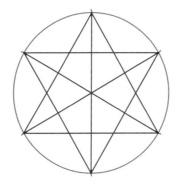

You will need:
• ruler
• compasses
• coloured pencils
• eraser

Then follow these steps to make your design.

• Erase the circle.

• Repeat the hexagonal pattern.

• Then erase some lines inside the first pattern.

• Finish with one of these two designs.

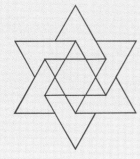
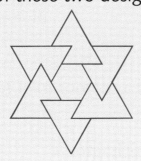

• Colour your pattern to make a shape that has a sense of rotation.

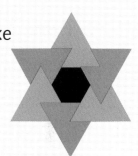

2 Start with a basic hexagonal pattern and make your own 'rotating' shape.

Using the basic hexagonal pattern, construct the designs below.

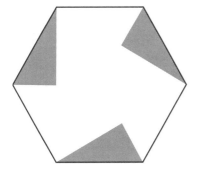
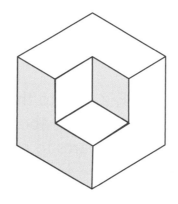

You will need:
• ruler
• compasses
• coloured pencils
• eraser

Connecting midpoints

Draw 2-D shapes accurately and use conventional markings for lines and angles

You will need:
- Resource 63: Connecting midpoints
- ruler

Challenges 1,2

1 In triangle ABC the midpoint of each side is marked by the letters D, E and F.

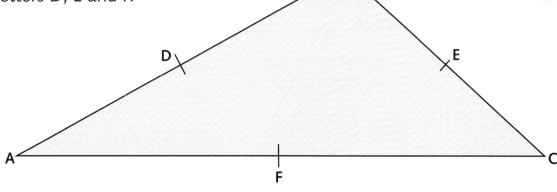

a Measure these lines to the nearest millimetre.

   i line AC   **ii** line AF   **iii** line FC

b Write the lines that are equal.

2 On Resource 63: Connecting midpoints, use your ruler to join the midpoints D and E.

a Measure the line DE to the nearest millimetre.

b Write what you notice about the lengths of the lines DE and AC.

Challenge 2

1 On Resource 63: Connecting midpoints, use your ruler to join the midpoints D and F.

a Measure the lines BC and DF to the nearest millimetre. Write what you notice about the two lengths.

b Measure ∠ABC, ∠ACB, ∠ADF, ∠AFD to the nearest degree. Write what you notice about the angles. Use single and double arcs to mark each pair of equal angles.

You will need:
- Resource 63: Connecting midpoints
- ruler
- protractor
- 1 cm squared paper

2 Draw a 12 cm by 6 cm rectangle on 1 cm squared paper.

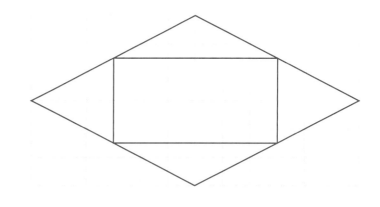

- Mark the midpoints of the sides of the rectangle and join them as in the diagram.
- Mark the midpoints of the sides of the rhombus and join them as in the diagram.

a Measure and calculate the perimeter of the inner and outer rectangles.

b Write what you notice about the two lengths.

3 Draw a different size rectangle on 1 cm squared paper. Join the midpoints in the same way you did in Question 2 until you have made the inner rectangle. Measure and compare the perimeters of the two rectangles you have drawn.

You will need:
- ruler
- 1 cm squared paper

1 On 1 cm squared paper, draw a parallelogram. Mark the midpoints of the sides of the parallelogram and join them. Then mark the mid points of the inner parallelogram and join them. Compare the perimeters of the the inner and outer parallelograms.

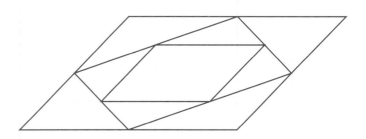

2 On 1 cm squared paper, draw an isosceles trapezium. Mark the midpoints of the sides of the trapezium and join them. Then mark the mid points of the inner shape and join them. Compare the perimeters of the inner and outer shapes.

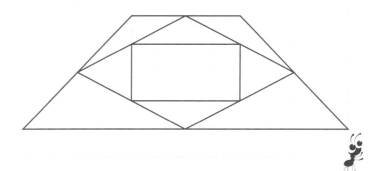

Multiplying decimals by a 2-digit number using the grid method

- Multiply a decimal by a 2-digit number using the grid method
- Estimate and check the answer to a calculation

Challenge 1

1 For each machine, work out the output number for each input number.

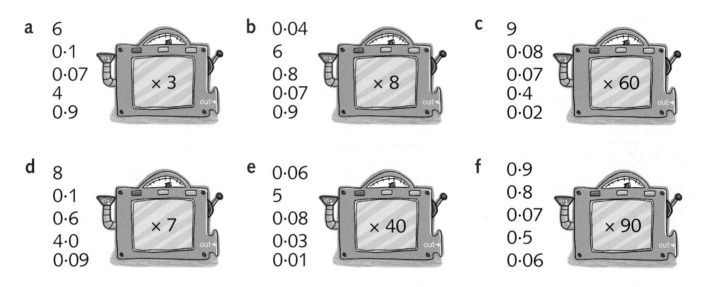

a
6
0·1
0·07
4
0·9
× 3

b
0·04
6
0·8
0·07
0·9
× 8

c
9
0·08
0·07
0·4
0·02
× 60

d
8
0·1
0·6
4·0
0·09
× 7

e
0·06
5
0·08
0·03
0·01
× 40

f
0·9
0·8
0·07
0·5
0·06
× 90

2 Calculate the total of the output numbers for each machine above.

3 Place the machines in order, smallest output total to largest output total.

4 Calculate the difference between the machine with the smallest and the machine with the largest total output.

5 Each of the machines above has been given a different multiplication function to complete. Multiply each output answer from the sets above by the number shown below to find the new answers.

- Set **a** – multiply by 60
- Set **b** – multiply by 10
- Set **c** – multiply by 50
- Set **d** – multiply by 40
- Set **e** – multiply by 70
- Set **f** – multiply by 20

Estimate the answer to each calculation. Then work out the answer using the grid method. Compare your answer with your estimate.

Example

$2.64 \times 38 \rightarrow 3 \times 40 = 120$

×	2	0·6	0·04
30	60	18	1·2
8	16	4·8	0·32

$$79\cdot20$$
$$+\ 21\cdot12$$
$$\overline{100\cdot32}$$
$$\small 1$$

a 3.46×35

b 6.71×93

c 5.45×84

d 3.86×45

e 8.26×25

f 5.75×43

g 8.65×19

h 7.35×18

i 3.28×28

j 9.83×47

k 2.67×89

l 9.07×34

m 4.89×16

n 1.89×57

o 6.47×36

p 8.18×81

Use each of the five digit cards once in each calculation in that box. Make a calculation that gives the answer shown.

1   3   5   7   9

0   2   4   6   8

a   .   ×   = 75·27

b   .   ×   = 126·75

c   .   ×   = 694·45

d   .   ×   = 93·60

e   .   ×   = 288·96

f   .   ×   = 36·12

Multiplying decimals by a 2-digit number using the expanded written method

- Multiply a decimal by a 2-digit number using the expanded written method of long multiplication
- Estimate and check the answer to a calculation

Challenge 1

What number is each clue describing?

a It is six times larger than 0·09.

b It is 0·6 more than triple 0·05.

c It is 100 times larger than 0·07 multiplied by 6.

d It is one quarter of 100.

e It is double 3·9 and double again.

f It is 10 less than when you multiply 50 by 0·5.

g It is 8 times more than 8·9.

h It is 10 times smaller than 0·5.

i It is half of 0·32 and half again.

j It is the sum of 7 multiplied by 0·07 and 0·25 multiplied by 4.

k It is the same as 2·22 multiplied by 4 add 3 multiplied by 3·33.

l It is 5 times larger than 2·3 multiplied by 2.

Challenge 2

Estimate the answer to each calculation. Then work out the answer using the expanded written method of long multiplication. Convert the decimals to whole numbers, carry out the calculation, then convert the answer back to a decimal.

a 2·38 × 25   **b** 4·55 × 46   **c** 6·84 × 31

d 5·78 × 56   **e** 6·74 × 28   **f** 8·76 × 15

g 3·45 × 19   **h** 2·78 × 35   **i** 6·38 × 42

j 6·74 × 27   **k** 7·35 × 18   **l** 3·98 × 51

m 8·06 × 37   **n** 5·40 × 75   **o** 9·38 × 19

Example

5·37 × 33 → 5 × 30 = 150

5·37 × 33 is equivalent to 537 × 33 ÷ 100.

```
          5  3  7
    ×        3  3
          2  1     (7 × 3)
          9  0     (30 × 3)
    1  5  0  0     (500 × 3)
          2  1  0  (7 × 30)
          9  0  0  (30 × 30)
    1  5  0  0  0  (500 × 30)
    1  7  7  2  1
       1     1
```

17,721 ÷ 100 = 177·21

5·37 × 33 = 177·21

1 Work out the total cost of each purchase. Write your answer in pounds (£).

a 13 boxes of eggs costing £3.59 each.

b 29 bottles of juice costing £2.89 each.

c 46 burgers costing £5.38 each.

d 38 pizzas costing £6.29 each.

e 54 cupcakes costing £1.96 each.

f 25 bottles of olive oil costing £4.85 each.

g 17 loaves of bread costing £2.49 each.

h 94 milkshakes costing £3.26 each.

i 67 pencils costing £0.79 each.

j 78 chocolate bars costing £1.95 each.

2 Work out the total cost of each purchase. Think carefully about how you are going to work out the answer: using a mental or a written method. Write your answer in pounds (£).

a 18 books costing £8.55 each.

b 62 pies costing £5.90 each.

c 43 bags of popcorn costing £3.70 each.

d 39 coffees costing £4.80 each.

e 76 sandwiches costing £4.10 each.

f 56 cans of soup costing £1.76 each.

g 38 large cakes costing £9.39 each.

h 27 bags costing £7.39 each.

i 69 candles costing £3.67 each.

j 48 pens costing £2.89 each.

31

Multiplying decimals by a 2-digit number using the formal written method

- Multiply a decimal by a 2-digit number using the formal written method of long multiplication
- Estimate and check the answer to a calculation

Challenge 1

1 Work out these calculations.

a 600 × 9	b 70 × 50	c 800 × 6	d 70 × 70
60 × 90	700 × 5	80 × 6	700 × 7
60 × 9	70 × 5	80 × 6	70 × 7
6 × 9	7 × 5	80 × 60	7 × 7
0·6 × 9	0·7 × 5	0·8 × 6	7 × 0·7
0·06 × 9	0·07 × 5	0·08 × 6	7 × 0·07

e 30 × 90	f 110 × 40	g 1,200 × 7
300 × 9	1,100 × 4	120 × 70
30 × 9	110 × 4	120 × 7
3 × 9	11 × 4	12 × 7
0·3 × 9	11 × 0·4	12 × 0·7
0·03 × 9	11 × 0·04	0·12 × 7

2 Write five multiplication calculations that give a total of each of the numbers below.

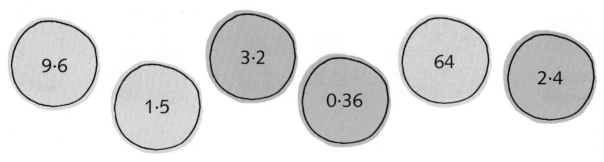

9·6   1·5   3·2   0·36   64   2·4

Estimate the answer to each calculation.
Then work out the answer using the formal
written method of long multiplication.
Convert the decimals to whole numbers,
carry out the calculation, then convert the
answer back to a decimal.

a 6.34×18

b 4.73×34

c 7.93×29

d 2.78×75

e 7.54×26

f 8.94×63

g 7.25×14

h 8.29×25

i 9.86×37

j 6.42×58

Example

$2.46 \times 38 \rightarrow 2 \times 40 = 80$

2.46×38 is equivalent
to $246 \times 38 \div 100$.

$$
\begin{array}{r}
2\ 4\ 6 \\
\times \quad 3\ 8 \\
\hline
1\ 9^3\ 6^4\ 8 \\
7^1\ 3^1\ 8\ 0 \\
\hline
9\ 3\ 4\ 8 \\
{\scriptstyle 1} \quad {\scriptstyle 1}
\end{array}
$$

$9{,}348 \div 100 = 93.48$

$2.46 \times 38 = 93.48$

Work out the answers to these problems. Take care – you will need to
use operations other than multiplication to calculate the answers.

a The sewing and fabric shop sells
reels of blue and red ribbon
each with 90 metres of ribbon
on them. The blue ribbon is
cut into pieces 2·25 metres in
length. The red ribbon is cut
into lengths of 1·25 metres.
How many more pieces of red
ribbon will there be?

b Bags of 10 buttons
cost £6.90. How
much would it cost
to buy 55 buttons?
How much change
would I receive
from £50?

c A length of fabric
measures 5·67 m
by 38 m. What
is the area of the
fabric?

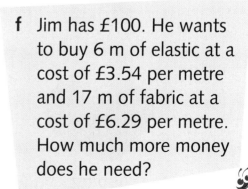

d Liz bought three
bags of sequins and
a reel of cotton.
The total cost was
£25.40. The reel of
cotton cost £3.56.
How much did each
bag of sequins cost?

e Ben bought 26 blue
zips and 39 purple
zips. He spent £247.39
altogether. Purple
zips cost £4.01 each.
How much does one
blue zip cost?

f Jim has £100. He wants
to buy 6 m of elastic at a
cost of £3.54 per metre
and 17 m of fabric at a
cost of £6.29 per metre.
How much more money
does he need?

Solving word problems (4)

- Solve problems involving addition, subtraction, multiplication and division
- Interpret remainders according to the context

Challenge 1

Multiply each pair of numbers to find the number above.
The first one has been done for you.

a [9.6]
[8] [1·2]

b [ ]
[7] [0·9]

c [ ]
[6] [0·08]

d [ ]
[9] [3·7]

e [ ]
[4·3] [6]

f [ ]
[14] [0·07]

g [ ]
[52] [0·3]

h [ ]
[19] [0·09]

i [ ]
[30] [0·8]

j [ ]
[6·5] [6]

k [ ]
[26] [0·07]

l [ ]
[38] [0·3]

m [ ]
[11] [0·11]

n [ ]
[25] [0·07]

o [ ]
[9·8] [0·1]

Challenge 2

Use the information below to work out the answer to each
of these questions, rounding your answers where appropriate.
Remember to use estimation to check your answers.

Biscuits:
£5.26 box

Chocolates:
£4.58 box

Pizza:
£9.38 each

Apples:
£1.47 pack of 3

Cupcakes:
£2.56 each

Soft drinks pack of 6:
£4.28

a Holly buys one dozen cupcakes. What is the total cost?

b Cupcakes are sold in packs of a dozen. The bakery department has 2,308 cupcakes to sell. How many packs can they make?

c If you buy 14 boxes of biscuits and 25 boxes of chocolates, how much do you spend?

d How much less does a box of chocolates cost than a box of biscuits?

e Gemma has invited 73 people to a party.
   i How many packs of soft drinks will she need to buy so that each guest can have one can?
   ii How much will she pay for these packs in total?

f If you buy 2 dozen apples altogether, what is the total cost?

g If you buy one of each item, how much money will you need?

h How much change from £100 would you receive if you bought 37 cupcakes?

i If you buy one pizza you get another one half price. If you buy 6 pizzas and pay with a £50 note, how much change will you receive?

j Apples come in packs of 3. Jerzy is making 13 apple pies and needs 4 apples for each pie.
   i How many packs does he need to buy?
   ii How much will he pay in total?

k A pack of one dozen cupcakes costs £25. How much money would you save by buying them in a pack rather than as 12 single items?

l There are 439 apples altogether.
   i How many packs of 3 can be made?
   ii If the supermarket sells half of the packs in one day, how much money would they take?

3 Make up your own word problems to match these calculations using the items in the pictures in Challenge 2.

    a $20 - (12 \times £1.47)$

    b $(£4.28 \div 4) \times 6$

    c $(10\% \times £5.26) \times 6$

    d $£2.56 \times 12 + £4.58 \times 11 + £4.28 \times 6$

    e $£100 \div £9.38$

    f $£50 < \boxed{} \times £1.47$

Fractions, factors and multiples (2)

- Use common factors to simplify fractions
- Use common multiples to express fractions with the same denominator

1 Simplify these fractions.

a $\frac{8}{10}$ b $\frac{10}{20}$ c $\frac{15}{25}$ d $\frac{9}{12}$ e $\frac{20}{28}$

f $\frac{12}{18}$ g $\frac{16}{24}$ h $\frac{24}{30}$ i $\frac{22}{26}$ j $\frac{21}{35}$

Example

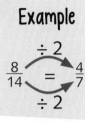

Both the numerator and the denominator have a factor of 2 so if I divide them both by 2 I get the simplified fraction $\frac{4}{7}$.

2 Write five fractions for your partner to simplify. Make sure you know the answers!

Example

1 Simplify these fractions in two different ways.

a $\frac{30}{40}$ b $\frac{28}{36}$ c $\frac{20}{40}$ d $\frac{18}{36}$ e $\frac{32}{44}$

f $\frac{18}{24}$ g $\frac{36}{44}$ h $\frac{45}{60}$ i $\frac{27}{45}$ j $\frac{48}{64}$

2 Choose two of these fractions and change them to fractions with the same denominator. Do this ten times. Fractions can be used more than once.

If I use the highest common factor, which is 10, I get the simplest fraction in one step.

$\frac{9}{20}$ $\frac{8}{15}$ $\frac{6}{10}$ $\frac{7}{12}$ $\frac{3}{5}$ $\frac{3}{14}$ $\frac{7}{9}$

$\frac{4}{7}$ $\frac{5}{8}$ $\frac{15}{24}$ $\frac{2}{6}$ $\frac{11}{18}$ $\frac{3}{4}$ $\frac{15}{28}$

3 Using the fractions in Question 2, can you find any sets of three fractions that can be changed to fractions with the same denominator?

4 Write three fractions that would simplify to the fractions below.
Use your knowledge of multiples.

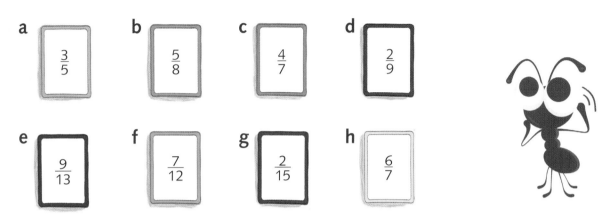

a $\frac{3}{5}$

b $\frac{5}{8}$

c $\frac{4}{7}$

d $\frac{2}{9}$

e $\frac{9}{13}$

f $\frac{7}{12}$

g $\frac{2}{15}$

h $\frac{6}{7}$

Challenge 3

1 Why does the mathematical rule for simplifying fractions state that you should use the highest common factor (HCF) of the numerator and denominator?

2 Work with a partner.

* Roll the dice four times and record your digits. If you roll a 0, count it as a 10.
* Use the digits to make two proper fractions.
* Look at the denominators. Convert the fractions to two fractions with a common denominator.
* Repeat three times.
* Now roll the dice six times and make three fractions. Convert these to three fractions with the same denominator.
* Repeat three times.

You will need:
• 0–9 dice

Adding and subtracting fractions (2)

Add and subtract fractions with different denominators and mixed numbers, using the concept of equivalent fractions

1 Work out these fraction addition and subtraction calculations.

> Remember with subtraction, you may need to exchange the first fraction even after you have made it into an equivalent fraction with a common denominator.

a $13\frac{1}{2} + 9\frac{3}{5}$

b $17\frac{2}{3} + 16\frac{3}{4}$

c $23\frac{1}{2} - 12\frac{1}{3}$

d $21\frac{4}{6} + 17\frac{2}{9}$

e $25\frac{3}{4} - 15\frac{7}{8}$

f $27\frac{2}{5} - \frac{1}{2}$

g $20\frac{7}{8} + 21\frac{3}{4}$

h $28\frac{4}{5} - 10\frac{1}{3}$

i $22\frac{2}{6} + 19\frac{1}{4}$

j $30\frac{1}{3} - 14\frac{5}{9}$

2 Work out these word problems.

a In my race I was in third place for $\frac{1}{4}$ of it, second place for $\frac{1}{3}$ of it, and then I was in the lead for the rest. For what fraction of the race was I in the lead?

b To prepare for the race, I ate a meal the night before which was $\frac{3}{5}$ carbohydrate and $\frac{1}{3}$ protein. The rest was vegetables. What fraction of my meal was vegetables?

c I started the race with a full water bottle. I drank $\frac{5}{8}$ and shared $\frac{1}{4}$ with my friend. What fraction of the water was left at the end of the race?

d My running shirt is red, white and green. It is $\frac{1}{2}$ white and $\frac{2}{5}$ red. What fraction of my shirt is green?

Challenge 1

1 Work out these fraction addition and subtraction calculations.
Write each answer in its simplest form.

a $36\frac{1}{2} - 25\frac{4}{5}$ b $31\frac{2}{6} - 19\frac{3}{4}$ c $28\frac{4}{9} + 20\frac{5}{6}$ d $33\frac{3}{7} + 21\frac{1}{2}$ e $28\frac{1}{10} - 11\frac{2}{3}$

f $42\frac{2}{3} + 18\frac{5}{7}$ g $46\frac{2}{6} - 31\frac{4}{5}$ h $29\frac{7}{10} + 37\frac{1}{4}$ i $35\frac{1}{4} - 26\frac{3}{5}$ j $43\frac{4}{9} + 21\frac{7}{12}$

2 Work out these word problems.

a In my next race I was in third place for $\frac{2}{5}$ of it, second for $\frac{2}{6}$ of it and then I was in the lead for the rest. For what fraction of the race was I in the lead?

b I started the race with a full water bottle. I drank $\frac{4}{9}$ and shared $\frac{2}{5}$ with my friend. What fraction of the water was left at the end of the race?

c My running shirt is blue, yellow and orange. It is $\frac{5}{8}$ blue and $\frac{1}{6}$ orange. What fraction of my shirt is yellow?

d When I was training for my race, I ran $7\frac{3}{4}$ km on one day and $12\frac{3}{5}$ km the next day.

i How far did I run altogether?

ii How much further did I run on the second day?

e After my race, I went out for pizza with my friends. We ordered 4 pizzas. I ate $1\frac{3}{10}$ of them, Sandy ate $1\frac{3}{4}$ and Chris ate the rest. How much did Chris eat?

1 After a race, £45,000 had been raised for four different charities. $\frac{2}{10}$ was given to a children's charity, $\frac{1}{3}$ to a homeless charity, $\frac{2}{5}$ to a sports charity and the rest to an animal charity.

a What fraction did the animal charity receive?

b How much money did each charity receive?

c One running club raised $\frac{2}{9}$ of the money and another running club raised $\frac{1}{12}$ of the money. How much did each of these two clubs raise for charity?

2 Write your own fraction problem about how money was raised for charity.
Give it to a partner to work out.

Fraction multiplication problems

Multiply simple pairs of proper fractions, writing the answer in its simplest form

Example

$$\frac{1}{5} \times \frac{2}{3} = \frac{1 \times 2}{5 \times 3} = \frac{2}{15}$$

Challenge 1

1 Multiply each pair of fractions.

a $\frac{1}{6} \times \frac{1}{2}$ b $\frac{1}{2} \times \frac{1}{4}$ c $\frac{1}{7} \times \frac{1}{3}$ d $\frac{1}{5} \times \frac{1}{2}$ e $\frac{1}{4} \times \frac{1}{3}$

f $\frac{2}{5} \times \frac{1}{3}$ g $\frac{2}{3} \times \frac{2}{4}$ h $\frac{1}{8} \times \frac{2}{3}$ i $\frac{2}{5} \times \frac{3}{4}$ j $\frac{3}{5} \times \frac{1}{5}$

2 Julie is going to make a cake but she only wants to use $\frac{1}{2}$ of the ingredients. Work out how much of each ingredient she needs.

Cake Recipe

$\frac{2}{3}$ cup of flour

$\frac{3}{4}$ cup of sugar

$\frac{1}{2}$ cup of butter

$\frac{1}{3}$ teaspoon of salt

Challenge 2

1 Multiply each pair of fractions, writing the answer in its simplest form.

Example

$$\frac{3}{5} \times \frac{4}{6} = \frac{3 \times 4}{5 \times 6} = \frac{12}{30} = \frac{2}{5}$$

a $\frac{3}{4} \times \frac{2}{5}$ b $\frac{2}{6} \times \frac{3}{7}$ c $\frac{3}{8} \times \frac{1}{2}$ d $\frac{4}{9} \times \frac{3}{6}$ e $\frac{5}{10} \times \frac{2}{4}$

f $\frac{1}{12} \times \frac{4}{5}$ g $\frac{7}{8} \times \frac{2}{3}$ h $\frac{6}{10} \times \frac{2}{6}$ i $\frac{5}{7} \times \frac{3}{7}$ j $\frac{3}{4} \times \frac{6}{8}$

2 Jonny is hungry. In the fridge he finds:

- $\frac{3}{8}$ of a pizza
- $\frac{3}{4}$ of a cake
- $\frac{4}{5}$ of a pint of milk
- $\frac{2}{3}$ of a bag of carrots

Write the answer to each of these problems in their simplest form.

a If he takes $\frac{1}{4}$ of each remaining amount, what fraction of the whole item will he have taken?

b If he eats half of each remaining amount, what fraction of each whole amount will be left?

c If he eats $\frac{2}{6}$ of each remaining amount, how much will he have eaten?

Challenge 3

For the following questions record your answers in a table like the one below.

	Sunday	Monday	Tuesday	Wednesday
Fraction of cereal eaten	$\frac{2}{10}$			
Fraction of cereal left	$\frac{8}{10}$			

On Sunday night the box of cereal had $\frac{8}{10}$ left in it.

a On Monday morning, Josie got up and ate some of the cereal. She ate $\frac{1}{4}$ of what was there and left $\frac{3}{4}$.

  i What fraction of the whole box of cereal did she eat?

  ii What fraction of the whole box of cereal did she leave?

b On Tuesday she ate $\frac{1}{2}$ of what was there and left $\frac{1}{2}$.

  i What fraction of the whole box of cereal did she eat?

  ii What fraction of the whole box of cereal did she leave?

c On Wednesday she ate $\frac{4}{6}$ of what was there, and left $\frac{2}{6}$.

  i What fraction of the whole box of cereal did she eat?

  ii What fraction of the whole box of cereal did she leave?

d Compare how much cereal was in the box on Sunday night to how much was in the box on Wednesday night.

Fraction division problems

Divide proper fractions by whole numbers

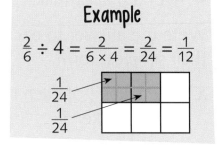

Example

$$\frac{2}{6} \div 4 = \frac{2}{6 \times 4} = \frac{2}{24} = \frac{1}{12}$$

$\frac{1}{24}$

$\frac{1}{24}$

Challenge 1

1 Work out these fraction division calculations.

a $\frac{2}{3} \div 4$

b $\frac{1}{6} \div 3$

c $\frac{2}{5} \div 3$

d $\frac{3}{4} \div 2$

e $\frac{1}{2} \div 5$

f $\frac{2}{6} \div 3$

g $\frac{3}{5} \div 4$

h $\frac{3}{8} \div 2$

i $\frac{4}{6} \div 3$

2 Four friends have these pizzas to share. How much of each pizza will each of them get?

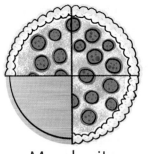

Margherita

Four cheese

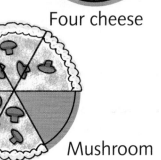

Mushroom

Challenge 2

1 Work out these fraction division calculations.
Make sure your answers are simplified.

a $\frac{3}{4} \div 5$ **b** $\frac{5}{8} \div 4$ **c** $\frac{6}{10} \div 3$ **d** $\frac{3}{7} \div 2$ **e** $\frac{4}{9} \div 3$ **f** $\frac{6}{8} \div 4$

g $\frac{4}{5} \div 3$ **h** $\frac{8}{10} \div 5$ **i** $\frac{3}{5} \div 9$ **j** $\frac{9}{10} \div 6$ **k** $\frac{11}{12} \div 3$ **l** $\frac{2}{9} \div 5$

2 Choose one of the calculations from Question 1 and draw a diagram to go with it.

42

3 Work out these word problems.

a Gemma has a piece of string. She cuts it so that she has $\frac{6}{8}$ of it and gives the rest to her brother. She uses her part to tie up five plants in her garden. What fraction of the original length of string does she use on each plant?

b The Cooper family have $\frac{5}{7}$ of a cake left.

  i What fraction of the whole cake will each of them get if they share it equally?

  ii Dad says, "As I made the cake, I think I should get extra, so count me as two people." How much would they each get if they agreed to do this?

c Six cats have found half a fish to share equally.

  i How much of a whole fish will each of them get?

  ii Luckily one of them then finds $\frac{3}{4}$ of another fish to share. What fraction of this whole fish will they get?

d Mrs Phillips has asked five children to stay in at lunch time to discuss their maths. She has half an hour with them. What fraction of an hour will each child have if she sees each child individually for the same length of time?

Work out these word problems.

a Colin the cook has $\frac{3}{8}$ kg of sugar. He bakes 5 cakes.

  i What fraction of a kilogram of sugar is in each cake?

  ii How many grams of sugar are in each cake?

b Colin has made pastry. He used 0·7 kg of flour. He rolls $\frac{4}{5}$ of it out into a long strip. He cuts this into eight pieces.

  i What fraction of the flour is in each piece?

  ii What mass of flour is in each piece?

c Colin has $\frac{6}{10}$ left of the pie he baked yesterday. Four customers have each just ordered a slice of pie.

  i What fraction of the whole pie would each of them get if what is left is shared equally?

  ii Before he serves his customers Colin decides he is hungry and would also like a piece of pie. What fraction of the whole pie will each of them get now?

Converting units of capacity

Convert between millilitres and litres using decimals up to 3 places

1 Write each capacity using decimal notation.

a **i** $\frac{4}{10}l$ **ii** $\frac{4}{100}l$ **iii** $\frac{4}{1,000}l$

b **i** $\frac{9}{10}l$ **ii** $\frac{9}{100}l$ **iii** $\frac{9}{1,000}l$

Example

$\frac{1}{10}l = 0{\cdot}1\ l$

$\frac{1}{100}l = 0{\cdot}01\ l$

$\frac{1}{1,000}l = 0{\cdot}001\ l$

2 Convert each capacity to litres using decimal notation.

a **i** 300 ml   **ii** 30 ml   **iii** 3 ml

b **i** 700 ml   **ii** 70 ml   **iii** 7 ml

c **i** 1,600 ml   **ii** 160 ml   **iii** 16 ml

Example

100 ml = 0·1 l

10 ml = 0·01 l

1 ml = 0·001 l

3 Convert each capacity to millilitres.

a **i** 0·8 l **ii** 0·08 l **iii** 0·008 l

b **i** 4·5 l **ii** 4·05 l **iii** 4·005 l

1 Convert the millilitres of rain water in each bucket to litres then round your answer to 1 decimal place.

Example

4,545 ml = 4·545 l ≈ 4·5 l

a 5,727 ml   **b** 8,070 ml    **c** 3,704 ml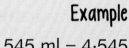

d 16,364 ml    **e** 18,095 ml    **f** 11,507 ml

2 Convert each capacity to millilitres.

    a 4·9 *l*   **b** 4·49 *l*   **c** 9·04 *l*   **d** 0·94 *l*   **e** 40·909 *l*   **f** 94·004 *l*

3 For each statement, work out the answer to each part and write whether the statement is true or false.

    a $\frac{1}{2}$ of 3 *l* > $\frac{1}{4}$ of 5 *l*   **b** $\frac{1}{2}$ of 1·5 *l* < $\frac{1}{4}$ of 2 *l*

    c $\frac{1}{3}$ of 1 *l* > $\frac{2}{3}$ of 900 ml   **d** $\frac{1}{4}$ of 1 *l* < $\frac{1}{5}$ of 750 ml

    e $\frac{1}{3}$ of 1·8 *l* > $\frac{3}{4}$ of 1,200 ml   **f** $\frac{4}{5}$ of 4 *l* < 10,000 ml

4 Copy and complete this pattern as far as you can go.

                 10 litres – 999 ml = 9·001 litres

                9·001 litres – 999 ml =   litres

                     litres – 999 ml =   litres

5 You pour one or two of the amounts of water on the right into an empty 1 litre measuring jar. Write in litres the seven **different** amounts of water that your jar could now have in it.

    250 ml   0·1 *l*   50 ml   0·25 *l*

allenge 3

Dr Davies has four measuring jars labelled A, B, C and D and four test tubes labelled 1, 2, 3 and 4. Each measuring jar is filled with a different liquid and each test tube is filled with a different chemical. She transfers the liquid from one measuring jar and the chemical from one test tube into an empty jug and mixes them together. How many different combinations of liquid and chemical can she make?

Maritime problems

Convert between units of capacity to solve problems using decimal notation

Challenge 1

Each goldfish needs a minimum of 9 litres of water.

1 How many goldfish can be kept in the tanks at the marine centre with these capacities:

    a 90 litres   **b** 135 litres   **c** 180 litres   **d** 216 litres

2 What is the capacity in litres for the tank that the marine centre will need for:

    a 12 goldfish?   **b** 25 goldfish?

3 The water level in a tank for 10 goldfish has fallen to 87·25 litres. How many litres of water must be added to the tank to bring it up to the minimum capacity for the goldfish?

Challenge 2

1 Andy sells motor boat fuel and refuels boats. He writes each sale in his record book. Copy and complete Andy's entry.

Boat	Meter reading at fuel pump (*l*)		Fuel sold (*l*)
	Before sale	After sale	
Sea Wind	6,658	6,756	98
Sea Breeze	6,756	6,930	
Sea Eagle	6,930		158
Sea Sprite		7,225	137
Sea Hawk		7,391	166

2 Water is leaking from a tap at the marine centre at the rate of 5 ml per second.

    a If a 1 litre jug is placed under the tap, how many seconds will it take to fill the jug?

    b If the tap continues to leak at the same water-flow rate, how much water will be lost:

      i in one hour?   **ii** in one day?

3 The drinks machine at the marine centre café mixes 200 ml of syrup with 800 ml of water.

    a How many litres of water are needed to mix with 4,500 ml of syrup?

    b How many litres of syrup are needed to mix with 64 litres of water?

4 The Sea Queen has two fuel tanks.

Tank 1
1,076·175 *l*

Tank 2
895·358 *l*

    a How many litres of fuel altogether are in the Sea Queen's tanks?

    b How much more fuel is in Tank 1 than in Tank 2?

    c The Sea Queen draws alongside to refuel. It needs 4,500 litres altogether for the day's trip to the island. How many litres of fuel are added to Tank 1 and Tank 2 so that each tank holds the same amount?

allenge
3

Tanya is a marine biologist. She filled ten 500 ml bottles with samples of sea water. She capped the ten bottles and placed them in a rack made up of 25 sections so that no line (horizontal, vertical or diagonal) had more than 1 litre of liquid.

Use 1 cm squared paper to mark off a 5 × 5 square grid. Draw circles in the grid to show how Tanya could have placed her ten bottles in the rack. Write a statement explaining your reasoning.

You will need:
• 1 cm squared paper
• ruler

Volume of cubes and cuboids

Calculate the volume of cubes and cuboids using the rule V = *lbh*

1 Each cube is made with 1 cm³ cubes. Calculate the volume of these cubes using the rule V = *lbh*.

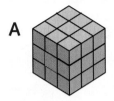  

A   B   C

Example

V = *lbh*

= 2 × 2 × 2

= 8 cm³

2 The arrows show the length, breadth and height of each cuboid. Calculate the volume of these cuboids using the rule V = *lbh*.

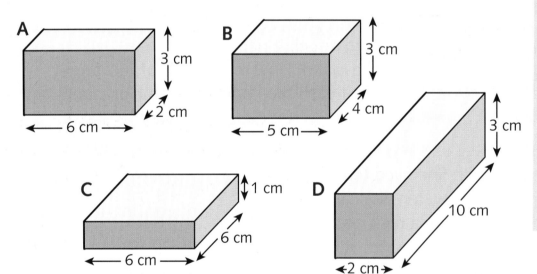

A — 3 cm, 2 cm, 6 cm
B — 3 cm, 4 cm, 5 cm
C — 1 cm, 6 cm, 6 cm
D — 3 cm, 10 cm, 2 cm

Example

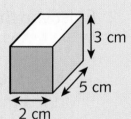

3 cm

5 cm

2 cm

V = *lbh*

= 5 × 2 × 3

= 30 cm³

1 Calculate the volume of these cubes and cuboids using the rule V = *lbh*.

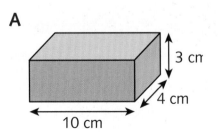 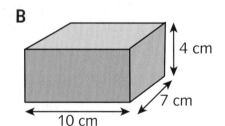 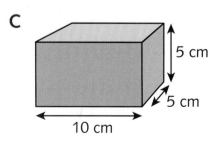

A — 3 cm, 4 cm, 10 cm
B — 4 cm, 7 cm, 10 cm
C — 5 cm, 5 cm, 10 cm

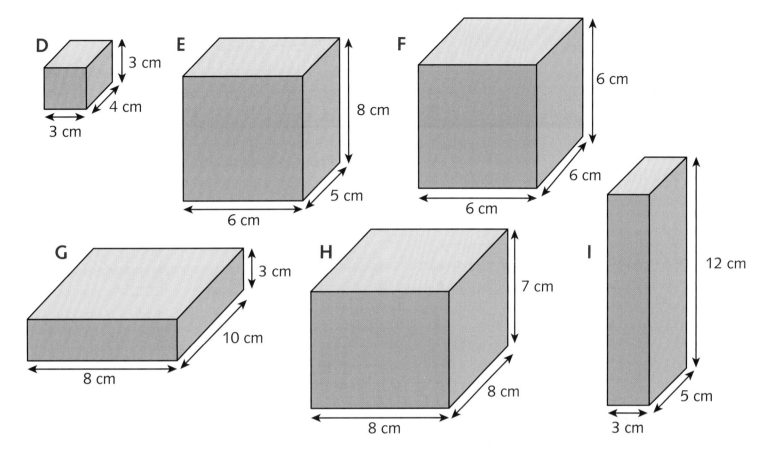

2 Calculate the volume of these large containers in cubic metres. Write them in order, smallest to largest.

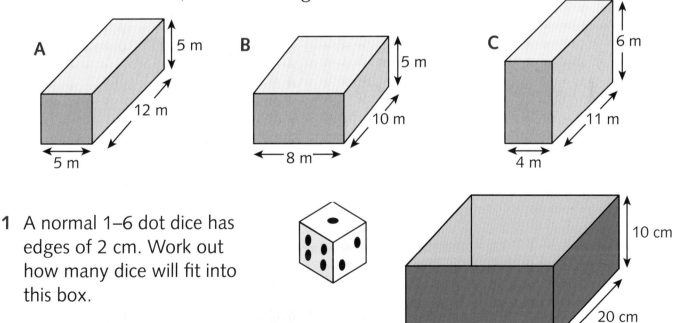

1 A normal 1–6 dot dice has edges of 2 cm. Work out how many dice will fit into this box.

2 A cube has edges of 4 cm. Draw a diagram of a cuboid that will hold 100 of these cubes. Label the dimensions to show its length, breadth and height.

Calculating volume and finding missing lengths

Calculate the volume of cubes and cuboids and find unknown lengths

Challenge 1

Copy the table below. Use the rule $V = lbh$ to calculate the volume.

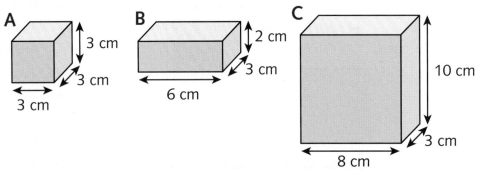

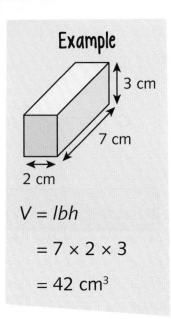

Example

$V = lbh$

$= 7 \times 2 \times 3$

$= 42 \text{ cm}^3$

Cuboid	Length (cm)	Breadth (cm)	Height (cm)	Volume (cm³)
A				
B				
C				

Challenge 2

1 The volume is shown for each cuboid below. Work out the unknown length for each cuboid.

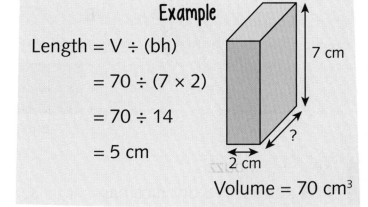

Example

Length = $V \div (bh)$

$= 70 \div (7 \times 2)$

$= 70 \div 14$

$= 5 \text{ cm}$

Volume = 70 cm³

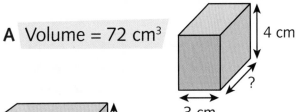

A Volume = 72 cm³

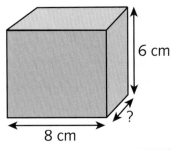

B Volume = 144 cm³

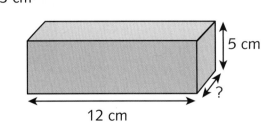

C Volume = 180 cm³

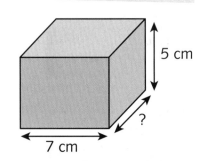

D Volume = 245 cm³

2 Each cuboid below has a volume of 120 cm³. Work out the unknown dimension for each cuboid.

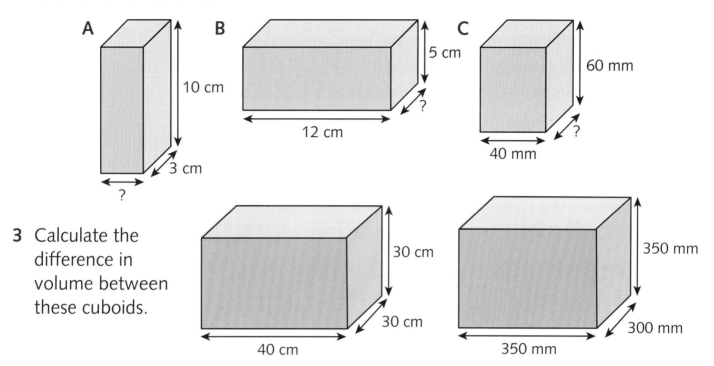

3 Calculate the difference in volume between these cuboids.

4 Calculate the difference in volume between these fish tanks.

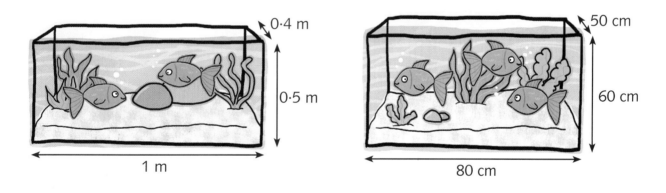

Read each puzzle then work out the values for the unknown measurements for each shape described.

a My height is 5 m. My volume is 165 m³. What is my length and breadth if they are prime numbers?

b My volume is 273 mm³. All my measurements are odd numbers. What are they?

c One of my edges is 6 cm. My volume is 216 cm³. My other two edges are equal in length. What do they measure?

d My volume is 336 cm³. My measurements are three 1-digit consecutive numbers. What are they?

BODMAS

Use knowledge of the order of operations to carry out calculations involving the four operations

 Challenge 1

1 Work out these calculations using the BODMAS rule.

a 24 + 67 × 2

b (125 – 50) × 3 ÷ 5

c 5 × 8 + 61

d (180 ÷ 10) × 4 + 99

e 3 × 5 + 49 ÷ 7

f 72 – 9 ÷ 9

g 72 ÷ 8 + (24 × 5)

h (43 × 3) + (121 ÷ 11)

i 153 – (67 + 23)

j (7 × 12) + (5 × 13)

k 49 ÷ 7 + 36

l (23 + 24) × 6 – 135

m (72 × 2) – (72 ÷ 4)

n 165 + (15 × 6) – (128 ÷ 8)

2 Choose five of the calculations from Question 1 and put the brackets in a different place to get a different answer.

> **Rule**
>
> The order for operations is:
> - **B** **B**rackets
> - **O** **O**rders (e.g. 4^2)
> - **DM** **D**ivision and **M**ultiplication
> - **AS** **A**ddition and **S**ubtraction
>
> The way to remember this is: **BODMAS**

Challenge 2

1 Work out these calculations using the BODMAS rule.

a $10^2 – (20 × 3)$

b (350 – 15) + (20 × 7)

c 150 + (60 × 6)

d $(420 + 50) × (25 – 22)^2$

e (52 + 52) × (5 – 2)

f (43 + 7) × (137 – 132)

g (499 – 3) + (46 × 6)

h $(33 × 7) – (2 × 5)^2$

i 560 – (40 × 7)

j 783 – (10 × 9)

k (26 × 7) + (41 × 8)

l (425 – 213) + (47 × 3)

m 368 – (11 × 14)

n $(287 – 187)^2 – 453 + (2,000 – 75)$

o $4,500 – (3 × 4)^2$

2 Choose five of the calculations from Question 1 and put the brackets in a different place to get a different answer.

3 Using only the digits 1, 3, 5, 6 and 8, along with any of the four operations and brackets, make each of the numbers below. Can you find different ways to make these numbers?

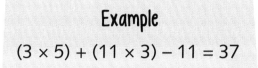
Example
$(3 \times 5) + (11 \times 3) - 11 = 37$

 37

 65

 70

 142

 Challenge 3

1 Work out these calculations using the BODMAS rule.

a $547 + 262 - 520 \div 10$

b $5 \times 13 + 99 - 7^2$

c $(85 \div 5) \times 12 + 62$

d $42 \times (12 + 6 - 5)$

e $62 \times (15^2 - 2)$

f $3{,}920 + (23 \times 4) \div 2$

g $7 \times 13^2 + (957 - 279)$

h $6 \times 8^2 + 4{,}258$

i $583 - 17^2 + (348 \div 6)$

j $288 \div (4 \times 6 + 8)$

k $19^2 - (4 \times 7) \times 3$

l $6{,}054 + (76 \times 4) \div 4 - 869$

m $(482 - 108) \div (16 + 6)$

n $6{,}238 - 70^2 + (4{,}628 \times 2)$

o $6{,}316 - 16^2 - (847 \div 11)$

2 Using only the digits 2, 4, 5, 7 and 9, along with any of the four operations and brackets, make each of the numbers below. Can you find different ways to make these numbers?

 59

 87

 41

 93

160

BODMAS challenge

Use knowledge of the order of operations to carry out calculations involving the four operations

 Challenge 1

Can you make all the numbers from 1 to 20 using the four operations, brackets and the number 3?

Example

$(3 + 3) \div 3 = 2$

 3 ÷ +  (−) ×

 Challenge 2

Use the table below and the rules of BODMAS to work out the answers to the calculations and find the names of five well-known mathematicans.

1	2	3	4	5	6	7	8	9	10	11	12	13
A	B	C	D	E	F	G	H	I	J	K	L	M

14	15	16	17	18	19	20	21	22	23	24	25	26
N	O	P	Q	R	S	T	U	V	W	X	Y	Z

Once you have all the letters, you will find the name of a mathematician!

1 $(50 \times 50) \div 25 - (10 \times 8)$ $(46 \times 32) \div 23 \div 4$

$(156 + 65) - (298 - 85)$ $65 \times 9 + 7^2 - 627$

$375 - (48 + 240) - 72$ $(75 + 69) \div 12 + 6$

$400 - (99 + 282)$ $9^2 - (224 \div 4)$ $156 \times 2 \div (464 - 152)$

Hint

If a box is blue, it means you will need that letter twice.

2 $(278 + 135) \times 2 - 803$ $(50 \times 50) \div 25 - (10 \times 8)$ $(630 \div 5) \div 3^2$

$675 - (180 + 240) - 240$ $(921 - 436) \div (776 \div 8)$

3 $(50 \times 50) \div 25 - (10 \times 8)$ $724 - (941 - 220)$ $156 \times 2 \div (464 - 152)$

$96 \div (2^2 \times 6)$ $400 - (99 + 282)$ $(75 + 69) \div 12 + 6$

$(921 - 436) \div (776 \div 8)$

4 $96 \div (2^2 \times 6)$ $(75 + 69) \div 12 + 6$ $435 + 380 + 900 - 1{,}706$

$117 \times 2 \div (591 - 573)$ $(921 - 436) \div (776 \div 8)$ $400 - (99 + 282)$

$(156 + 65) - (298 - 85)$ $724 - (941 - 220)$ $476 + (513 \div 3) - 646$

5 $435 + 380 + 900 - 1{,}706$ $375 - (48 + 240) - 72$ $(630 \div 5) \div 3^2$

$72 \times 3 \div (591 - 555)$ $(386 + 275) - (699 - 40)$ $156 \times 2 \div (464 - 152)$

$724 - (941 - 220)$

6 Now make up some calculations to spell the name of these mathematicians.
Remember to use brackets.

| Turing | | Euclid | | Euler | | Fermat |

allenge 3 Play this game with a partner.

* Shuffle the cards and place them face down in a pile.
* Turn over four cards. If a 2 is turned over it stands for 'the power of 2'.
* Using all four digits on the cards and adding brackets and any operations, each person makes a calculation and works out the answer.
* Keep the calculation a secret and only tell the other player your answer.
* You both now try to work out each other's calculation.
* Score a point if you work out the calculation correctly.
* Play ten times, and the winner is the one with the most points.

You will need:
* Resource 1: 0–9 number cards

Number puzzles

Solve problems involving addition, subtraction, multiplication and division

Challenge 1

Answer each calculation, writing your answer in the Challenge 1 number puzzle on Resource 80.

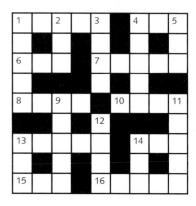

Across

1 33,296 + 7,429

4 6,000 – 5,243

6 2,448 ÷ 3

7 38,000 + 29,000

8 1,563·5 + 2,078·5

10 5,309 + (47 × 7)

13 22,158 + 36,258

14 3,610 ÷ 5

15 79 × 10

16 43,963 – (1,284 × 2)

Down

1 56,359 – 8,536

2 84 × 9

3 5,065 + 699

4 72,492 + (451 + 73)

5 74,000 ÷ 100

9 47,985 – 585

11 122,936 – 35,691

12 10,000 – 2,366

13 (121 + 68) × 3

14 37 × 19

Challenge 2

Answer each calculation, writing your answer in the Challenge 2 number puzzle on Resource 80.

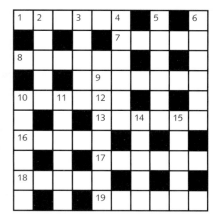

Across

1 537,645 – 58,263

7 39,327 + (158 × 6)

8 6,521·06 × (356 – 256)

9 17,098,300 ÷ (62 + 38)

10 366,757 + 416,259 + 499

13 604,628 – 12,000

16 80 × (547 – 247)

17 800,000 – 56,000

18 16,758 × 4

19 1,000,018 – 19

Down

2 59,254·48 + 17,263·52

3 (962 – 291) × (97 – 52)

4 39,024 + 21,488 + 185,647

5 32,689 + 92,894 + 2,353

6 474,430 – 2,695 – 14,367

10 802,003 – 59,635

11 343,988 – 43,988

12 26,880 + 65,045 + 58,804

14 77,085 – 48,666

15 5,785 + 18,254

Answer each calculation, writing your answer in the Challenge 3 number puzzle on Resource 80.

Across

8 $81,265 - 59,000$

9 $12,157,384 - 3,560,000$

10 $5,384,197 + (414 \div 46)$

11 $6,420,000 \div 10^2$

12 $504,986 - 34,400$

13 $72,934 \times (100 \div 10)$

15 $151,040 + 555,555$

17 $354,295 + 270,623$

20 $24,713 + 3,654$

22 $9,205,479 - (989 - 239)$

Down

1 27×45

2 $4,268 \times 100$

3 $75,426,887 - (2^2 + 2^2)$

4 $3,923 \times 20$

5 $9^2 \times 36$

6 $308,205 - 68,992$

7 $25,380,084 + 3,659,215 + 5,066,749$

12 $169,255 + 307,967$

14 $424 \times (281 + 244)$

16 $365 \times (152 \div 8)$

18 $46,160 - 36,588$

19 $3,588 \div 6$

21 $1,638 \div (3 \times 7)$

23 $6,587,125 - 6,587,026$

Curious questions

Solve problems involving addition, subtraction, multiplication and division

Work with a partner.

- Together, choose the curious question you would like to find a solution to.
- Together, think about the following:
  - What do you already know that can help you find the solution?
  - What do you need to find out and use to help you?
  - How will you go about finding the solution? (There might be more than one way!)

  Choose the best option and try it.

- Make sure you stop to review the process as you work through the question.
- When you've found a solution:
  - Carefully check what you have done.
  - Think about how well you did. Could you have done it a better way?
  - Write a report giving your solution and describing the process you went through to arrive at your solution.
  - Write a statement about what you have learned from this.
- If there's time, choose another curious question to investigate.

Challenge 1

500,000

1 How long is 500,000 seconds?

2 How far is 500,000 centimetres?

3 How many cups would 500,000 millilitres of water fill?

4 How long would it take to write your name 500,000 times?

Challenge 2

1,000,000

1 How far would 1,000,000 pencils laid end to end stretch?

2 How long is 1,000,000 minutes?

3 How high is a stack of 1,000,000 ten pences?

4 How long would it take to count to 1,000,000?

5 How far is 1,000,000 paces?

6 Write a curious question for others in your class to solve. Write a statement justifying why it would be of interest to your class to find a solution to this problem.

Challenge 3

2,000,000

1 How old would you be if you have lived for 2,000,000 minutes?

2 What size container would you need to hold 2,000,000 beads?

3 How far would 2,000,000 paperclips laid end to end stretch?

4 How long does it take for your heart to beat 2,000,000 times?

5 Research some curious questions that mathematicians have spent time working out.

What can you find out about Fermat's last theorem? How long did it take to solve it?

Flora and fauna proportion problems

Recognise and solve proportion problems

Challenge 1

1 A survey of British amphibians gave the results shown in the table. Calculate the proportion of each amphibian as a percentage.

You will need:
- calculator

Amphibian	Frog	Common Toad	Natterjack toad	Great-crested newt
Number seen	25	12	8	5

2 A conservation group raised funds to plant some native British deciduous trees. They purchased and planted 60 trees in total, a mixture of oak, ash and beech.

The proportion of oak trees is 50%, the proportion of ash trees is 20% and the proportion of beech trees is 30%.

Calculate the number of each species of tree.

Challenge 2

1 A survey of woodland animals gave the results shown in the table. Calculate the proportion of each animal as a percentage.

Animal	Badger	Fox	Hedgehog	Rabbit	Squirrel
Number seen	33	55	44	77	66

2 A conservation group raised funds to plant some native British evergreen trees. They purchased and planted a mixture of yew, Scots pine and holly.

Of all the trees, 0·2 are yew, 0·4 are Scots pine and the remainder are holly.

There are 44 holly trees.

a Calculate the number of yew and Scots pines.

b What is the total number of trees?

3 A survey of reptiles gave the results shown in the table. Calculate the proportion of each animal as a decimal and as a percentage.

British reptiles	Common lizard	Slow worm	Adder	Grass snake	Smooth snake
Number seen	81	69	39	51	60

4 A keen entomologist has been keeping a record of the large beetles observed in his local area for five years. He thought that the proportion of stag beetles was increasing.

Year	Total number of large beetles seen	Number of stag beetle sightings
2010	1,200	18
2011	1,400	21
2012	800	16
2013	1,400	28
2014	1,000	25

a Calculate the proportion of stag beetles for each year.

b Is the proportion of stag beetles increasing? Explain your reasoning.

allenge 3

1 A survey of butterflies gave the results shown in the table.

1,500 butterflies were counted.

Calculate how many of each species of butterfly was seen.

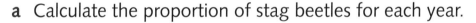

Butterflies	Tortoiseshell	Common blue	Red admiral	Brimstone	Peacock
Percentage seen	24%	18%	26%	14%	18%

2 A conservation group raised funds to plant some native British hedges. They purchased and planted a 200 metre hedge comprising a mixture of hawthorn, hazel and holly. There are 3 hedge plants per metre.

11 in every 20 hedge plants are hawthorn, 25% are hazel and the rest are holly.

Calculate the total number of hedge plants and the number of each species.

Scale factor and ratio problems

- Understand and use ratio to solve problems
- Solve problems involving scale factors

Challenge
1

1 A TV company plans its evening schedules in the following ratios:

Films and drama : Comedy and quiz shows : News and current affairs = 4 : 2 : 3

An evening runs from 6:00 p.m. to midnight. There are 120 minutes of 'News and current affairs' each evening. Find the number of minutes for:

a Films and drama

b Comedy and quiz shows

2 Work out the answer to each question.

a 8 apples cost £3.60, how much will 5 apples cost?

b 3 mangoes cost £3.90, how much will 4 mangoes cost?

c 12 lemons cost £3.00, how much will 7 lemons cost?

d 2 pineapples cost £3.70, how much will 3 pineapples cost?

You will need:
- 1 cm squared paper
- ruler

Challenge
2

1 Draw each of the shapes described below on 1 cm squared paper and then enlarge each one with a scale factor of 2.

a 2 cm square

b 1 cm × 4 cm rectangle

c right-angled triangle with the right angle between sides of length 2 cm and 3 cm.

2 Work out the answer to each question.

a 12 oranges cost £2.88, how much will 5 oranges cost?

b 4 figs cost £3.40, how much will 3 figs cost?

c 3 grapefruit cost £2.04, how much will 4 grapefruit cost?

d 5 bananas cost £1.15, how much will 9 bananas cost?

e 6 limes cost £1.74, how much will 7 limes cost?

3 Here are some facts about a school of 450 children. Find the ratios and change them to their simplest forms. You will need to use your answer to Question **a** to work out Questions **b** and **c**.

a 200 of the 450 children are boys. Find the ratio of boys to girls.

b 75 girls play in a netball or hockey team. Find the ratio of 'girls in a team : girls not in a team'.

c 75 boys play in a football or cricket team. Find the ratio of 'boys in a team : boys not in a team'.

d 150 children walk to school. Find the ratio of 'children who walk : children who do not walk'.

e 200 children learn a musical instrument. Find the ratio of 'children who play a musical instrument : children who do not play a musical instrument'.

f Investigate some of these ratios for your school.

4 A large supermarket chain has 1,035 stores throughout Britain.

a 20% of the stores have a petrol station attached. How many stores is this?

b 1 in 3 stores has an in-store bakery. Of the stores with a bakery, 2 out of every 5 has a café attached. How many stores are there with both a bakery and café?

Challenge 3

1 Look at this selection of flags from countries in Africa. Estimate the ratio of the area of each colour for each flag. Some are harder than others.

You will need:
- 1 cm squared paper
- ruler
- coloured pencils

a Nigeria

b Republic of Congo

c Rwanda (*Don't include the yellow sun)

d Uganda (*Don't include the crested crane)

e Cape Verde (*Don't include the yellow circle of stars)

2 Using squared paper, design your own flag using three colours in the ratios 2 : 1 : 5.

*Although you are not including the details for the maths task, they are important features of the flags. The crane is the national symbol of Uganda and it is standing on one leg to symbolise that the country is not stationary, but moving forward. The sun on the Rwandan flag represents enlightenment. The circle of ten stars on the Cape Verde flag portrays the ten main islands.

Building and jewellery ratios

Solve missing value ratio problems using multiplication and division

Challenge 1

1 A bracelet manufacturer makes bracelets with beads arranged in repeating patterns. The total number of beads in a bracelet must be within the range 15–20.

Using × and ○ to represent two types of beads, draw two possible bracelet designs with the following ratios:

a 1 : 2   **b** 3 : 1

2 A builder has laid some patios using cream and grey coloured slabs. The ratio of cream to grey slabs in the designs is 2 : 3. Calculate the number of grey slabs and the total number of slabs for designs with:

a 8 cream slabs   **b** 20 cream slabs   **c** 36 cream slabs

Challenge 2

1 A necklace manufacturer makes necklaces with beads arranged in repeating patterns. The total number of beads in a necklace must be within the range 40–60.

   a Using × and ○ to represent two types of beads, draw two possible necklace designs with the ratio 2 : 3.

   b List the exact number of beads that can be used to make necklaces for each of the ratios below.

      i 3 : 5   **ii** 2 : 5   **iii** 1 : 8

2 A builder has to make concrete for a number of jobs.

   a Calculate how much sand and gravel he will need for each job if the ratio of cement : sand : gravel is 1 : 2 : 4.

      i To concrete in a bird table, he uses 3 buckets of cement.

      ii To concrete in a garden seat, he uses 4 bags of cement.

      iii To make a garden path, he uses 8 full wheelbarrows of cement.

b Using the same ratio of cement : sand : gravel, calculate how much sand he uses to make:

    i 14 full buckets of concrete to fix a new gate

    ii 35 full wheelbarrows of concrete to lay a base for a conservatory.

3 A new town has permission to build homes in the following proportions:

- 10% are large detached houses (D)
- 20% are town houses (T)
- 30% are semi-detached houses (S)
- 40% are apartments (A)

  a In Phase 1 of the building, there are 400 homes. Calculate how many of each type there are.

  b In Phase 2 of the building, there are 100 town houses. How many homes are there in Phase 2?

  c At the end of Phase 3, there are 380 town houses in total (Phases 1, 2 and 3). Calculate how many homes there are in the new town altogether.

allenge 3

1 A necklace manufacturer makes necklaces with three different types of beads arranged in repeating patterns. The total number of beads in a necklace must be within the range 50–80.

  a Using ×, ○ and □ to represent the beads, draw two possible necklace designs with the ratio 1 : 2 : 3.

  b List the exact number of beads that can be used to make necklaces for each of the ratios below.

    i 1 : 4 : 5   **ii** 3 : 4 : 6   **iii** 4 : 13 : 2

2 A builder has laid some patios using three sizes of slabs. The ratio of small : medium : large slabs in the designs is 3 : 5 : 1. Calculate the number of each size of slabs for designs with:

  a 18 small slabs   **b** 25 medium slabs   **c** 90 slabs

Tasty ratio and proportion problems

Use knowledge of fractions and multiples to solve ratio and proportion problems

Challenge 1

1 Here are the ingredients for two refreshing summer drinks:

Homemade lemonade – serves 4
- 3 lemons
- 140 g caster sugar
- 1·2 litres water

Homemade melon cooler – serves 6
- 500 g melon chunks
- 2 limes – zest and juice
- 100 ml apple juice
- 1·4 litres shop-bought lemonade

a Calculate the ingredients required to serve both recipes to 12 people.

b If you have 560 g sugar, how many people can have homemade lemonade?

c How many people can you serve if you make the melon cooler using 7 limes?

2 Three celebration cakes are decorated with 8 walnuts for every 3 cherries.

a The first cake has 24 walnuts. How many cherries does it have?

b The second cake has 12 cherries. How many walnuts does it have?

c The third cake has 55 walnuts and cherries in total. How many of each is this?

Challenge 2

1 Jason sorted a bag of sweets into their different colours, as shown in the diagram below.

a Giving your answer first as a decimal and then as a percentage, what proportion of the sweets are:

   i green?   **ii** brown?   **iii** red?

b Giving your answer in its simplest form, what is the ratio of these sweets?

   i brown : purple   **ii** green : purple   **iii** yellow : blue

2 Calculate how much flour is required in each of these apple recipes.

   a Apple crumble with 500 g apples and the apple to flour ratio equal to 10 : 3.

   b Apple crepes with 120 g apples and the apple to flour ratio equal to 12 : 5.

   c Apple and date loaf with 80 g apples and the apple to flour ratio equal to 4 : 11.

3 On his birthday Peter brings a large tin containing 48 biscuits to share with his class. There are 30 children in the class and each child eats one biscuit.

   a What proportion of the tin is eaten at school? Give your answer as a fraction, decimal and percentage.

   b He takes the remaining biscuits home to share with his family. After they each have one biscuit, 25% of the tin is left. How many people are in Peter's family?

4 An ice-cream manufacturer tries three new flavours: blueberry, peanut butter and pineapple. He makes the ice creams in the ratio 5 : 4 : 7.

   a The first week he has enough ice-cream to make 448 cones. How many cones of each flavour could he sell?

   b The next week he makes the same total number but in the ratio 3 : 2 : 3. How many more blueberry ice-cream cones could he sell in the second week?

1 A mug holds 240 ml. Eliza makes tea for herself and three friends. Calculate how many millilitres of milk there will be in each cup of tea when full.

   a Betty only likes a little bit of milk and her ratio is 1 part milk to 7 parts tea.

   b Carol likes her tea in the ratio of 3 parts milk to 7 parts tea.

   c Daisy likes her tea in the ratio of 1 part milk to 5 parts tea.

   d Eliza has a cup of tea in the ratio of 2 parts milk to 3 parts tea.

2 There are 96 children in Year 6. Work out how many children chose each vegetable as their favourite.

Hint

Look carefully at each sector of the pie chart and make approximations.

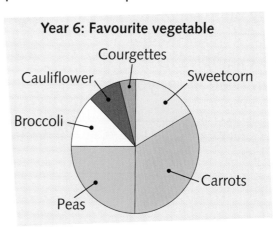

Year 6: Favourite vegetable

Using coordinates to locate shapes (2)

Use coordinates to describe the position of shapes in all four quadrants

Challenge 1

1 The grid shows the coordinates of eight red cars in a car park. Write the coordinates of cars A to H.

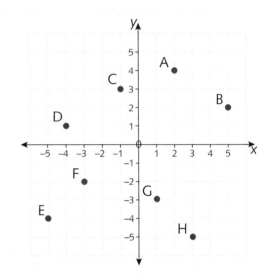

2 The exit from the car park is at the point (0, 4). Write the letter of the car that is:

- nearest to the exit
- furthest from the exit.

Challenge 2

1 Harry takes the penalty kicks for his rugby team.

- The kick is a drop goal if the ball goes over the bar and between the posts.
- The kick is a miss if the ball goes under the bar or outside of the posts.

Copy and complete Harry's score sheet. The first two examples have been filled in for you.

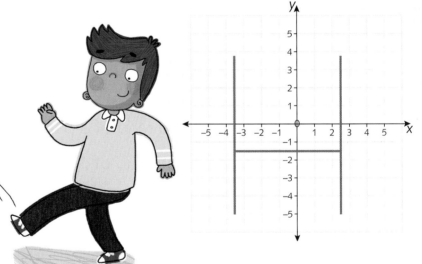

Coordinates of kick	(–1, 1)	(–4, –1)	(–3, 2)	(–4, 1)	(2, 0)	(–3, –2)	(–2, –1)	(0, 2)	(4, 2)
Result	Drop goal	Miss							

2 List the coordinates of:

   a rhombus ABCD

   b rectangle EFGH

3 In rectangle EFGH the points E, F and I form three vertices of a square. What are the coordinates of the fourth vertex J?

4 The points P, Q and R form three of the vertices of a parallelogram. What are the coordinates of the fourth vertex S?

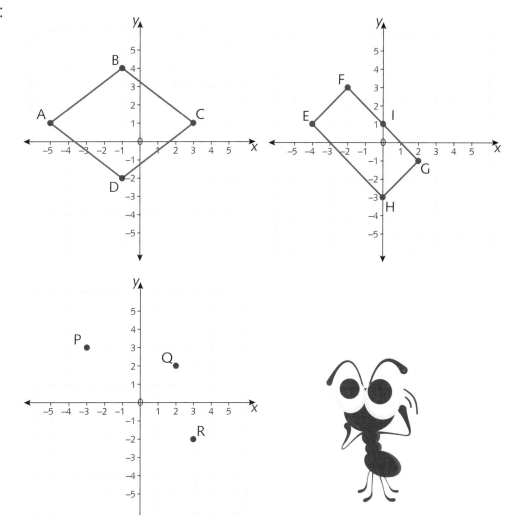

nallenge
3

Jan is writing a program for a robot to draw the net of a cube without going over the same line twice. She writes the coordinates of the vertices in order and makes this sketch of the route. Write the coordinates of the route from start to finish.

Example

Start: (−1, −2), (1, −2)…

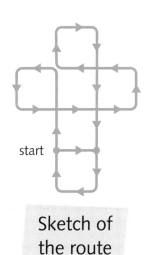

start

Sketch of the route

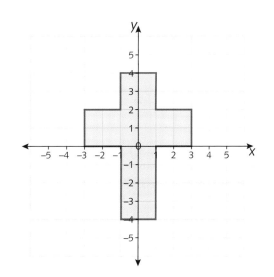

Plotting shapes in the four quadrants (2)

Plot and label shapes in the four quadrants and predict missing coordinates

Challenge 1

You will need:
- copies of Resource 12: 4-quadrant coordinate grids
- ruler

1 Plot these points onto a grid on Resource 12: 4-quadrant coordinate grids.

A (–3, 4)   B (–1, 1)   C (3, 3)   D (4, 0)

E (–4, –1)   F (–2, –4)   G (0, –2)   H (3, –5)

2 Write the letter of the point or points that are:

    a in the 2nd quadrant   **b** in the 3rd quadrant   **c** in the 4th quadrant

    d on the x-axis   **e** on the y-axis.

3 Using a ruler, join the points B, D, H and F in order to form a square.

Challenge 2

For each diagram, use a different grid on Resource 12: 4-quadrant coordinate grids.

1 Plot each point and join the points in order:

    a rectangle ABCD:
    A (–4, 2), B (3, 2),
    C (3, –2), D (–4, –2)

    b square EFGH:
    E (–1, 2), F (2, –1),
    G (–1, –4), H (–4, –1)

    c parallelogram JKLM:
    J (–2, 3), K (3, 1),
    L (3, –4), M (–2, –2)

    d rhombus PQRS:
    P (–1, 4), Q (1, 1),
    R (–1, –2), S (–3, 1)

2 The points A (–3, 1), B (3, 2) and C (4, –4) are three vertices of a square.

    • Plot the points and join them in order, A to B and B to C.

    • Find the coordinates of the missing vertex D.

    • Complete the drawing of the square.

3 The points E (–4, 1), F (–1, 4) and G (4, –1) are three vertices of a rectangle.

- Plot the points and join them in order, E to F and F to G.
- Find the coordinates of the missing vertex H.
- Complete the drawing of the rectangle.

4 The points J (–4, 1), K (3, 2) and L (5, –2) are three vertices of a parallelogram.

- Plot the points and join them in order, J to K and K to L.
- Find the coordinates of the missing vertex M.
- Complete the drawing of the parallelogram.

5 The points P (–1, 3), Q (1, 0) and R (–1, –3) are three vertices of a rhombus.

- Plot the points and join them in order, P to Q and Q to R.
- Find the coordinates of the missing vertex S.
- Complete the drawing of the rhombus.
- Find the coordinates for the intersection of the diagonals.

For each diagram, use a different grid on
Resource 12: 4-quadrant coordinate grids.

1 The line joining the points A (–4, 3) and C (2, –3)
is a diagonal of square ABCD.

- Plot the points A and C.
- Predict the missing coordinates for the
  vertices B and D.
- Complete the drawing of the square.

2 The line joining the points E (–3, 1) and F (3, 3) is a side of square EFGH.

- Plot the points E and F.
- Predict the missing coordinates for the vertices G and H if both points
  have negative y–coordinates.
- Complete the drawing of the square.
- Write the coordinates of the intersection of the diagonals at the point J.

Using coordinates to translate shapes (2)

Use coordinates to translate shapes and predict missing coordinates

The rectangle ABCD has been translated
5 squares to the right and 3 squares up.
We can write this as: $x + 5, y + 3$.

For both rectangles write the coordinates
for each vertex.

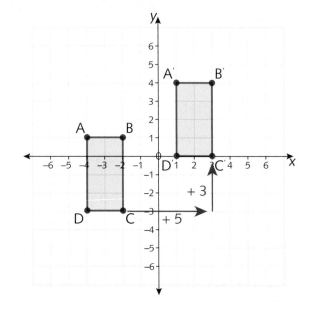

A $(-4, 1) \rightarrow$ A' $(1, \quad)$

B $(\quad, \quad) \rightarrow$ B' $(\quad, \quad)$

C $(\quad, \quad) \rightarrow$ C' $(\quad, \quad)$

D $(\quad, \quad) \rightarrow$ D' $(\quad, \quad)$

1 Copy the square EFGH onto a grid on Resource 12: 4-quadrant
coordinate grids.

a Draw where the square will be after the
translation $x + 4$.

b Write the coordinates for each vertex
of both squares.

You will need:
- Resource 12: 4-quadrant
  coordinate grids
- ruler

E $(\quad, \quad) \rightarrow$ E' $(\quad, \quad)$

F $(\quad, \quad) \rightarrow$ F' $(\quad, \quad)$

G $(\quad, \quad) \rightarrow$ G' $(\quad, \quad)$

H $(\quad, \quad) \rightarrow$ H' $(\quad, \quad)$

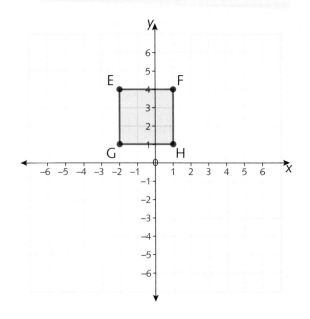

c On the same grid draw where the square
will be after the translation $y - 5$. Write
the coordinates for each vertex of both
squares as in Question **b** above.

2 Copy shape KLMN onto a grid on Resource 12: 4-quadrant coordinate grids.

    a Draw where the shape will be after the translation $x - 5$, $y - 3$.

    b Write the coordinates for each vertex of both shapes.

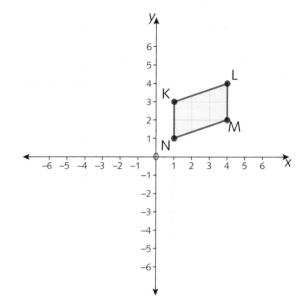

K (,   ) → K' (,   )

L (,   ) → L' (,   )

M (,   ) → M' (,   )

N (,   ) → N' (,   )

3 Copy shape PQRS onto a grid on Resource 12: 4-quadrant coordinate grids.

    a Draw where the shape will be after the translation $x + 6$, $y - 4$.

    b Write the coordinates for the vertices of both shapes.

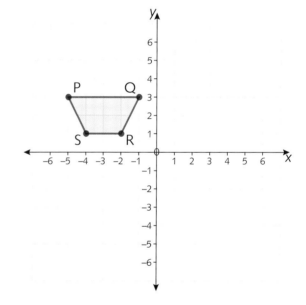

P (,   ) → P' (,   )

Q (,   ) → Q' (,   )

R (,   ) → R' (,   )

S (,   ) → S' (,   )

Challenge 3

Use the letters x and y to describe how each shape A has been translated to B.

a

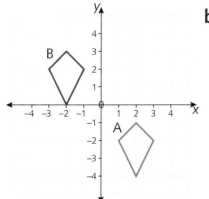

b

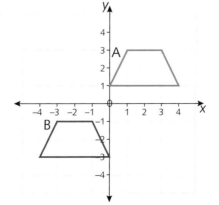

c

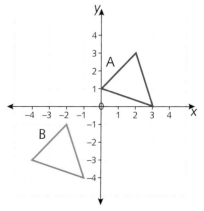

Four quadrants reflection

Use coordinates to reflect shapes into all four quadrants

You will need:
- Resource 12:
  4-quadrant
  coordinate grids
- ruler

Copy each shape onto a different grid on Resource 12:
4-quadrant coordinate grids. Reflect each shape first in
the y-axis then reflect both shapes in the x-axis.

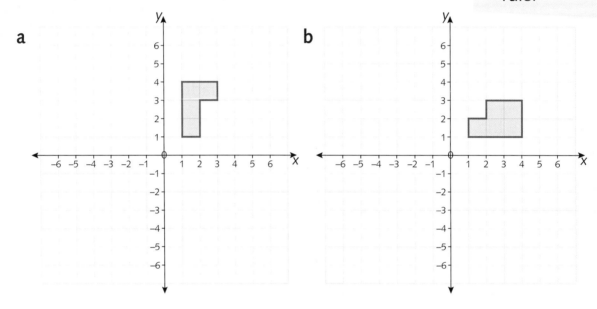

1 For each diagram, use a different grid on Resource 12: 4-quadrant
coordinate grids. Reflect each shape first in the y-axis then reflect
all of the shapes in the x-axis.

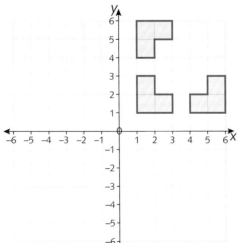

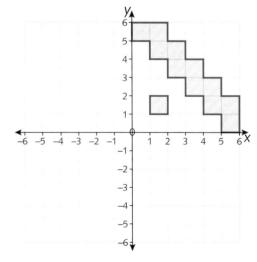

c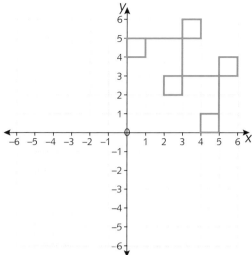

d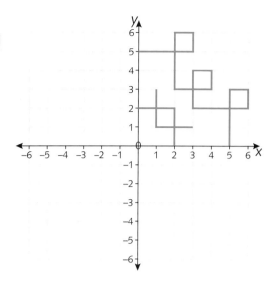

2 Copy the kite ABCD onto a grid on Resource 12: 4-quadrant coordinate grids.

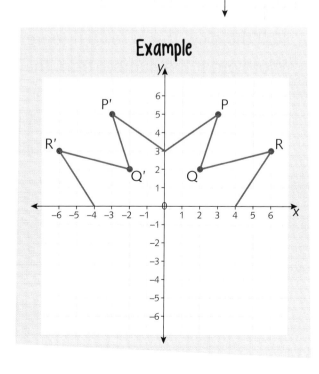

a Draw the reflection of the kite in the y-axis and then reflect both shapes in the x-axis.

b Write the coordinates for these points and their images.

A (,), A' (,), A" (,), A''' (,)

B (,), B' (,), B" (,), B''' (,)

C (,), C' (,), C" (,), C''' (,)

D (,), D' (,), D" (,), D''' (,)

Use Resource 12: 4-quadrant coordinate grids.

a Draw your own design in the first quadrant of one of the grids. Label three points P, Q and R.

b Draw the reflection of your design in the y-axis and then reflect both shapes in the x-axis.

c Write the coordinates for the vertices P, Q and R and their images as shown in Question **b**.

Example

Using divisibility tests

Use knowledge of multiples and factors to conduct tests of divisibility

Challenge 1

1 Use the tests of divisibility to write five numbers that are:

a between 300 and 600, and divisible by 5

b between 450 and 550, and divisible by 4

c between 400 and 450, and divisible by 3

d between 900 and 1,300, and divisible by 6

e between 4,000 and 5,000, and divisible by 9

f between 1,200 and 2,000, and divisible by 8

Rule

Tests of divisibility

A number is divisible by:

2 if the ones digit is even (0, 2, 4, 6 or 8).

3 if the sum of all its digits is a multiple of 3.

4 if the tens and ones digits are a multiple of 4.

5 if its ones digit is 0 or 5.

6 if it is even and is also divisible by 3.

8 if half of it is divisible by 4 or if its last three digits are a multiple of 8.

9 if the sum of all its digits is a multiple of 9.

10 if the ones digit is 0.

25 if the tens and ones digits are 25, 50, 75 or 00.

2 Look at the grid below.

- Choose a number from the grid and write it down.
- Roll the dice. If you roll 0 it represents 10.
- Work out if the number from the grid is divisible by the number rolled on the dice.
- If the number is divisible, draw a tick (✓) beside it. If not, draw a cross (✗).
- Your teacher will tell you how many numbers to choose.

You will need:
- 0–9 dice

62	523	142	287	83
34	618	864	43	2,592
192	71	66	924	216
1,677	759	353	864	3,938
75	1,728	89	497	5,184
32	890	804	2,580	21

I chose 759 and I rolled a 3. 759 is divisible by 3 so I've drawn a tick.

The boxes below have lost their labels. Use the divisibility tests on the opposite page to find which set of multiples are in each box. However, one number in each box does not belong. Find the number that does not belong and write it down. Then complete the label for each box.

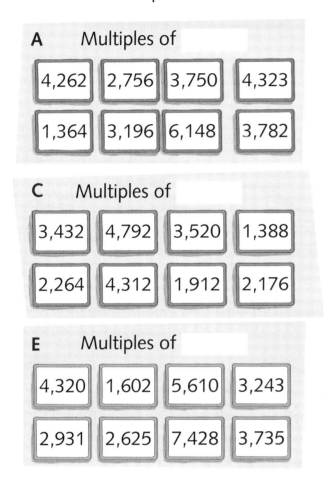

A Multiples of

| 4,262 | 2,756 | 3,750 | 4,323 |
| 1,364 | 3,196 | 6,148 | 3,782 |

C Multiples of

| 3,432 | 4,792 | 3,520 | 1,388 |
| 2,264 | 4,312 | 1,912 | 2,176 |

E Multiples of

| 4,320 | 1,602 | 5,610 | 3,243 |
| 2,931 | 2,625 | 7,428 | 3,735 |

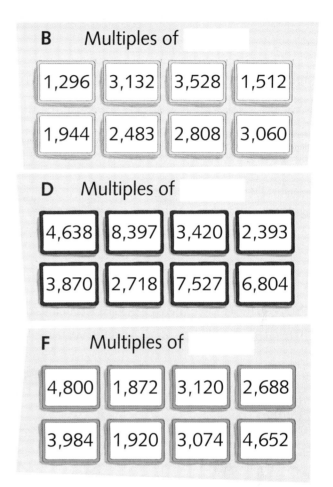

B Multiples of

| 1,296 | 3,132 | 3,528 | 1,512 |
| 1,944 | 2,483 | 2,808 | 3,060 |

D Multiples of

| 4,638 | 8,397 | 3,420 | 2,393 |
| 3,870 | 2,718 | 7,527 | 6,804 |

F Multiples of

| 4,800 | 1,872 | 3,120 | 2,688 |
| 3,984 | 1,920 | 3,074 | 4,652 |

Use your knowledge of divisibility tests to answer these questions.
For each question, explain how you know.

a Leap years occur every 4 years. Will the year 2072 be a leap year?

b Write a list of all the leap years that will occur in the 21st century.

c Is it possible to make complete octagons using 3,768 sides?

d A crate is filled with boxes of apples. There are 8 apples in each box. Could the total number of apples be 7,504?

e 25 pictures per second are transmitted to television sets. This means that in 3 minutes, 4,500 pictures are transmitted. Could this be true?

f There are 4 gills in a pint. Could full pints be made using 6,596 gills?

Review multiplication and division of whole numbers

- Use appropriate methods to multiply and divide whole numbers
- Estimate and check the answer to a calculation

Challenge 1

Look at the start number. Follow the instructions on the cards to find the final number.

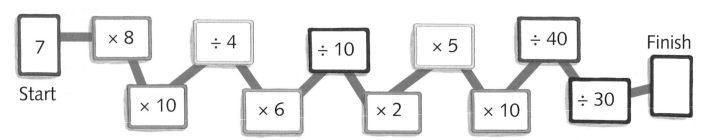

7 — × 8 — ÷ 4 — ÷ 10 — × 5 — ÷ 40 — Finish

Start

× 10 — × 6 — × 2 — × 10 — ÷ 30

Challenge 2

1 Sort these calculations into two groups: those that you can calculate using mental methods and those where you need to use a written method.

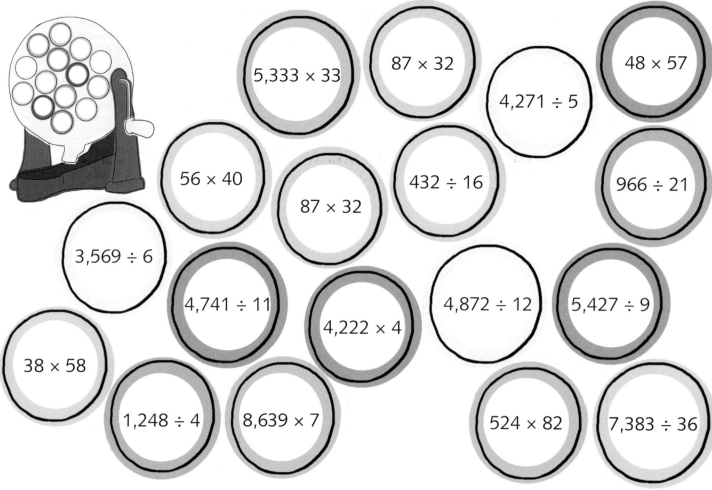

5,333 × 33

87 × 32

4,271 ÷ 5

48 × 57

56 × 40

87 × 32

432 ÷ 16

966 ÷ 21

3,569 ÷ 6

4,741 ÷ 11

4,222 × 4

4,872 ÷ 12

5,427 ÷ 9

38 × 58

1,248 ÷ 4

8,639 × 7

524 × 82

7,383 ÷ 36

2 Work out the answer to each calculation in Question 1. For the calculations that need a written method, use the most appropriate written method and show your working. Remember to estimate the answer first and then use your estimate to check your answer.

1 The children in Little Fishes Swimming Team swim every day to keep healthy and to train for competitions.

a Copy and complete the table to find out the distance they swim in the different time periods.

	Time period				
	1 day	**1 week**	**1 fortnight**	**June and July**	**1 year**
Julie	8 km				
Janice		42 km			
Justin			126 km		
Jarod	12 km				
Jasmeen		63 km			

b Make up five questions related to the information in your table. Include questions that use the four operations. Give your questions to a partner to solve.

2 Use the most appropriate method to work out the answer to each of these calculations: mental or written. Be sure to estimate and check your answers.

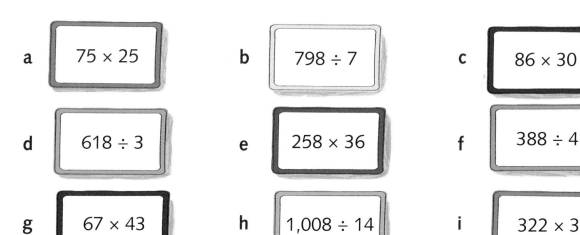

a 75 × 25

b 798 ÷ 7

c 86 × 30

d 618 ÷ 3

e 258 × 36

f 388 ÷ 4

g 67 × 43

h 1,008 ÷ 14

i 322 × 3

Review multiplication and division of decimal numbers

- Use appropriate methods to multiply and divide decimals
- Estimate and check the answer to a calculation

Challenge 1

Work out the answers to these calculations.

a | 52 × 10
b | 5·4 × 10
c | 630 × 10
d | 3·8 × 10

e | 6·3 × 100
f | 8 × 100
g | 3,600 ÷ 10
h | 24 ÷ 10

i | 560 ÷ 100
j | 3,600 ÷ 100
k | 36 × 1,000
l | 48,000 ÷ 1,000

Challenge 2

1 Sort these calculations into two groups: those you can calculate using mental methods and those where you need to use a written method.

6 × 0·3

5·46 ÷ 6

4·72 × 3

61·2 ÷ 18

36·8 ÷ 4

0·76 × 5

33·3 × 8

88·8 ÷ 24

53·43 ÷ 13

5·42 × 43

8·2 × 4

2 Work out the answer to each calculation. For the calculations that need a written method, use the most appropriate written method and show your working. Remember to estimate the answer first and then use your estimate to check your answer.

Answer these word problems. Remember to round answers involving money to 2 decimal places.

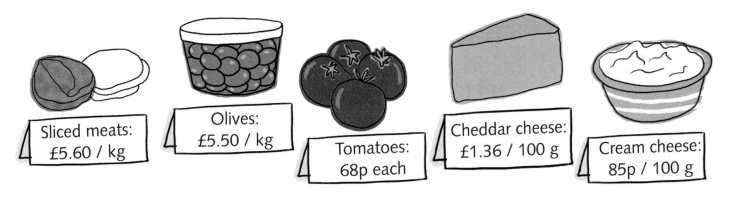

Sliced meats: £5.60 / kg

Olives: £5.50 / kg

Tomatoes: 68p each

Cheddar cheese: £1.36 / 100 g

Cream cheese: 85p / 100 g

1 Joseph makes his lunch for the working week (5 days). He buys 375 g sliced meat, 240 g cream cheese and 5 tomatoes.

   i   How much does he spend in total?

   ii On average, how much does he spend per day?

2 William buys his lunch every day, Monday to Friday. He buys a 320 g tub of olives and 1 tomato per day. How much does he spend per week?

3 Use the information from Questions 1 and 2 to answer these questions.

   i   Who spends the most on their lunch per day, Joseph or William?

   ii What is the difference in the amount they each spend per day?

   iii What is the difference in the amount they each spend per week?

4 If you bought 5 tomatoes and 500 g of each other item, how much change would you receive from £20?

5 The delicatessen uses 10 g each of sliced meat, Cheddar cheese, cream cheese and olives as filling on one of its sandwiches. Approximately how much do the fillings cost per sandwich?

6 Ron has £5 to spend on tomatoes. How many tomatoes can he buy?

7 A meat, Cheddar cheese and tomato sandwich costs £3.85. How many of these sandwiches can be bought for £20?

8 The delicatessen cuts each tomato into 5 slices. If it charged customers per slice, approximately how much would each slice cost?

Solving word problems (5)

- Solve problems involving addition, subtraction, multiplication and division
- Use estimation to check answers to calculations

Work out the unknown numbers.

a 2·6 ×  = 260

b 3·02 ×  = 302

c 9·7 ×  = 97

d 4·5 ×  = 45

e 1·18 ×  = 118

f 0·77 ×  = 77

g 22·2 ×  = 222

h 0·59 ×  = 59

i 7·09 × 100 =

j  × 100 = 311

k 0·03 × 100 =

l  × 10 = 2·1

m 3·19 ×  = 31·9

n  × 100 = 46

o 0·21 ×  = 21

1 For each of these questions, first estimate the answer and then work it out. Then compare your answer with your estimate. (Remember to round answers involving money to 2 decimal places.)

a The children in Year 6 decorate the school hall with balloons and streamers. Balloons cost £2.64 per bag of 8 balloons. Streamers cost £3.87 per roll. They decorate the hall with 6 rolls of streamers and 96 balloons. What is the total cost?

b Mrs Wu orders 65 pizzas for the Year 6 end-of-year party. The total cost is £620.10. How much does each pizza cost? If each pizza is divided into 8 slices, approximately how much does 1 slice cost?

c Mr Scott buys 70 party hats. They cost 25p each. How much does he spend? Give your answer in pounds.

d £500 is set aside to buy cupcakes. Cupcakes are sold in packs of 6. Each pack costs £5.59. Year 6 order 342 cakes altogether. How much money do they have left?

e Balloons cost £2.64 for a bag of 8. How much does 1 balloon cost? How much do 4 balloons cost?

f Mrs Sant buys 32 large bottles of juice. Each bottle costs £5.92. How much does she spend? If 6 cups of juice can be made from each bottle, approximately how much does it cost per cup?

g Using the information from all of the relevant questions, calculate how much Year 6 and their teachers spent on the party.

h The school contributes 25% of the total cost of the party. Local businesses donate 10% and the parents donate the rest. How much do the parents donate?

i Individual cupcakes cost £1.28 each. Packs of 6 cupcakes cost £5.59. How much money would you save by buying the pack of 6 cupcakes rather than 6 individual cupcakes?

2 What operation is represented by each ☆?

a (372 ☆ 6) ☆ 9 = 558   **b** (372 ☆ 6) ☆ 9 = 248   **c** 372 ☆ 6 ☆ 9 = 2,241

d 372 ☆ 6 ☆ 9 = 71   **e** 372 ☆ (6 ☆ 9) = 24·8   **f** 372 ☆ 6 ☆ 9 = 2,223

Challenge 3

1 Make up five of your own word problems about an end-of-year party. Use the ideas below to help you as well as using some of your own ideas. Swap your word problems with a friend to solve.

Disco entry ticket: £3.50   Face painting: £4.85   Prize: £35 voucher

Drinks: £1.75   Pizza slice: £0.95   Fries: £2.40

2 Using each digit only once per question, make each of the following calculations correct.

 1   4   7

 2 6

a ＿ × ＿ = 3,952   **b** ＿ ÷ ＿ = 29·5

c ＿ + ＿ = 803   **d** ＿·＿ ÷ ＿ = 4·8

e ＿·＿ × ＿ = 724·2   **f** ＿·＿ − ＿·＿ = 4·64

Percentages and prices

- Solve problems involving percentages

Challenge 1

The sports shop is closing down. The manager decides to reduce all of the items in the shop by 10% of their current price each day for the last three days that they are open: Monday, Tuesday and Wednesday. The percentage reduction is worked out on the price of the previous day. The prices shown below are before they are reduced. What will be the cost of each item on Wednesday?

£130

£50

£160

£30

£250

£80

Example

Monday
10% of £20 is £2
£20 − £2 = £18

£20

Tuesday
10% of £18 is £1.80
£18 − £1.80 = £16.20

Wednesday
10% of £16.20 is £1.62
£16.20 − £1.62 = £14.58

Challenge 2

1 The computer shop has a New Year sale, starting 1st January, for just 3 days. The manager reduces the prices by 10% each day. The percentage reduction is worked out on the price of the previous day. The prices shown below are before they are reduced. What will the prices be on 3 January?

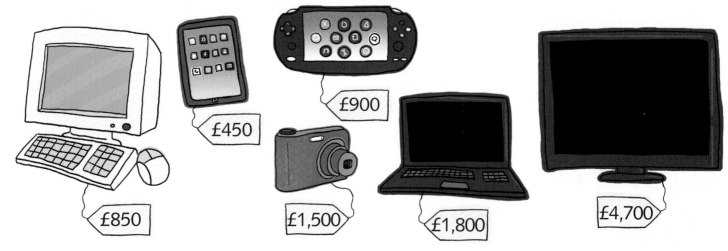

£450

£900

£850

£1,500

£1,800

£4,700

2 Would you rather buy the laptop on 2 January, or on 1 January with a 20% discount? Compare the prices and explain your reasons.

3 Would you rather buy the camera on 3 January, or on 1 January with a 28% discount? Compare the prices and explain your reasons.

Challenge 3

1 The supermarket is running a promotion: when you buy some items you will get an extra amount free. Work out what percentage of each item is free.

300 g for the price of 250 g

BISCUITS

WATER

1,200 ml for the price of 1,000 ml

525 g for the price of 500 g

RICE

690 g for the price of 600 g

1·1 kg for the price of 1 kg

CAT BISCUITS

1,190 g for the price of 850 g

POTATOES

429 ml for the price of 330 ml

2 Imagine you are a shop owner and want to sell all of your stock.

- How much will you reduce it by?
- Will you keep the same price each day or will you change it?
- Write a report about what you would do, explaining your reasoning and giving at least three worked examples.

Fractions, decimals and percentages (2)

- Recognise equivalences between fractions, decimals and percentages

Challenge 1

1 Copy each pair of fractions, decimals or percentages writing the correct symbol between them: < or > or =.

a $\frac{1}{2}$ 0·3

b 45% $\frac{1}{4}$

c 0·6 $\frac{7}{10}$

d $\frac{9}{10}$ 91%

e 0·75 $\frac{7}{10}$

f $\frac{7}{10}$ 0·65

g 55%   0·15

h 0·1 $\frac{1}{10}$

i 40% $\frac{2}{4}$

j $\frac{6}{10}$ 0·8

k $\frac{3}{4}$ 34%

l 20% $\frac{4}{10}$

2 Choose two of your answers from Question 1 and explain how you know your answer is correct.

3 For each set, put the fractions, decimals and percentages in order, smallest to largest.

a $\frac{1}{2}$ | 0·6 | 55% | $\frac{1}{4}$ | 0·2 | 23%

b 0·3 | 0·1 | 1% | 64% | $\frac{4}{5}$ | $\frac{1}{2}$

c $\frac{7}{10}$ | 0·4 | 35% | $\frac{1}{5}$ | 50% | 0·6

d $\frac{4}{5}$ | $\frac{3}{10}$ | 0·7 | 61% | 99% | $\frac{9}{10}$

4 Work with a partner. Each choose two different fractions, two different decimals and two different percentages from Question 3 and write them down. Work together to put them in order, smallest to largest.

Challenge 2

1 Copy each set of fractions, decimals or percentages, writing the correct symbol between them: < or > or =.

a 13% $\frac{1}{3}$

b 30%   0·03

c $\frac{7}{10}$ 0·71

d 0·25 $\frac{2}{5}$

e 52%   0·5

f $\frac{1}{5}$ 50%

g 80% $\frac{4}{5}$

h 0·14   44%

i $\frac{8}{20}$ 0·4

j $\frac{5}{8}$ 60%

k 0·06 $\frac{1}{20}$

l 5%   0·05

m 61%   0·66

n 0·16 $\frac{1}{6}$

o 66%   0·6

p $\frac{8}{20}$ 40%

2 Work out each of these lengths in centimetres.

a $\frac{8}{20}$ m   **b** 40% of a metre   **c** 0·52 m

d $\frac{3}{5}$ m   **e** $\frac{7}{10}$ m   **f** 16% of a metre

3 Work out each of these masses in grams.

a 34% of a kilogram   **b** 0·65 kg   **c** $\frac{3}{8}$ kg

d 72% of a kilogram   **e** 0·99 kg   **f** $\frac{23}{50}$ kg

4 Give an example of when it would be better to express something as a fraction rather than as a decimal or as a percentage. Explain your reasoning.
Give an example of when it would be better to express something as a percentage rather than as a decimal or as a fraction. Explain your reasoning.

Challenge 3

1 Work with a partner.

- Cut up the 19 cards on Resource 71: Fraction, decimal and percentage cards.
- Using the three blank cards, make different fraction, decimal and percentage cards.
- Put the < symbol on the table.
- Shuffle the cards and deal the cards out between you.
- The first person lays a card on one side of the < symbol.
- The second person must lay a card on the other side that is mathematically correct.
- The first person can then lay a card on top of either of the cards that are there, keeping the statement mathematically correct.
- Keep going until all the cards are used up.
- Repeat the activity, this time putting the inequalities symbol on the table so that it reads: >.

You will need:
- Resource 71: Fraction, decimal and percentage cards
- scissors

2 Design your own activity or game involving fractions, decimals and percentages using the cards from Resource 71.

Fraction and decimal equivalents (3)

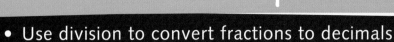

- Use division to convert fractions to decimals

Hint

Reducing a fraction to its simplest form can help you identify the decimal equivalent.

Challenge 1

1 Write the decimal equivalent for each of these fractions.

    a $\frac{1}{4}$ **b** $\frac{2}{5}$ **c** $\frac{7}{10}$ **d** $\frac{6}{8}$ **e** $\frac{3}{10}$

    f $\frac{4}{5}$ **g** $\frac{9}{10}$ **h** $\frac{2}{8}$ **i** $\frac{4}{20}$ **j** $\frac{6}{16}$

2 Copy this table.

Fraction	$\frac{1}{2}$	$\frac{1}{3}$	$\frac{1}{4}$	$\frac{1}{5}$	$\frac{1}{6}$	$\frac{1}{7}$	$\frac{1}{8}$	$\frac{1}{9}$	$\frac{1}{10}$
Decimal									

   a Fill in the decimal equivalents that you know.

   b Estimate the decimal equivalents that you do not know.

   c Work out the answers to the decimal equivalents you do not know. Check if your estimates were close.

Challenge 2

1 Estimate the decimal equivalent for each of these fractions.

   a $\frac{5}{8}$ **b** $\frac{5}{11}$ **c** $\frac{6}{6}$ **d** $\frac{7}{12}$ **e** $\frac{5}{9}$ **f** $\frac{1}{13}$

   g $\frac{6}{14}$ **h** $\frac{3}{7}$ **i** $\frac{11}{14}$ **j** $\frac{6}{15}$ **k** $\frac{9}{16}$ **l** $\frac{13}{15}$

2 Work out the decimal equivalents for the fractions in Question 1. Round each decimal to these degrees of accuracy:

   i 2 decimal places

   ii 3 decimal places

Example

$$\frac{6}{7} = 6 \div 7$$

$$\begin{array}{r} 0 \cdot 8\ 5\ 7\ 1 \\ 7\overline{)6 \cdot {}^{6}0\ {}^{4}0\ {}^{5}0\ {}^{1}0} \end{array}$$

   i 0·86   **ii** 0·857

3 Compare your estimates and the decimal equivalents from Questions 1 and 2. Which was your closest estimate? Why do you think that was?

4 The Williams family have made a cake.

- Dad ate 19% of the cake.
- The twins ate 0·15 of the cake each.
- Mum ate $\frac{1}{8}$ of the cake.
- Their brother ate $\frac{1}{5}$.

a Who ate the most cake?

b How much of the cake is left?

c How much of the cake did Mum and Dad eat altogether?

d How much of the cake did the three children eat altogether?

1 Work out the fraction and decimal equivalents for these percentages. Make sure the fraction is expressed in its simplest form.

You will need:
- calculator

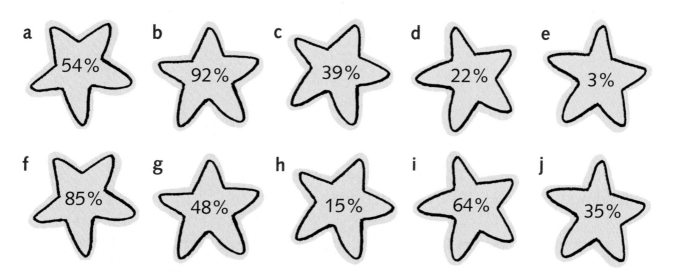

a 54% **b** 92% **c** 39% **d** 22% **e** 3%

f 85% **g** 48% **h** 15% **i** 64% **j** 35%

2 How many fractions can you find that have a decimal equivalent from 0·5 to 0·7? How will you start to investigate this? What do you already know that can help you?

Find the fractions

• Recognise fraction and decimal equivalences, checking equivalences using division

1 Copy and complete, writing the fractions that are equivalent to each decimal. Look carefully for any patterns or relationships between the fractions in each question.

Hint

Think about the relationship between the numerator and the denominator; e.g. if a fraction is equivalent to 0·5 the numerator is half the denominator.

a $0·1 = \frac{1}{10} = \frac{2}{20} = \frac{}{30} = \frac{}{40} = \frac{}{60} = \frac{}{100} = \frac{}{120} = \frac{}{140}$

b $0·5 = \frac{50}{100} = \frac{1}{2} = \frac{2}{4} = \frac{}{6} = \frac{}{24} = \frac{}{50} = \frac{}{62} = \frac{}{78} = \frac{}{80}$

c $0·25 = \frac{25}{100} = \frac{1}{4} = \frac{}{12} = \frac{}{20} = \frac{}{40} = \frac{}{52} = \frac{}{60} = \frac{}{80}$

d $0·8 = \frac{80}{} = \frac{}{10} = \frac{}{20} = \frac{}{30} = \frac{}{40} = \frac{}{50} = \frac{}{60} = \frac{}{70}$

2 Check that all your fractions in Question 1 are equivalent.

Example

$\frac{1}{10} = 1 \div 10 = 0·1$

1 Write four fractions that are equivalent to each of these decimals. Check that all your fractions are equivalent to the decimal by dividing the numerator by the denominator.

a 0·2   **b** 0·6   **c** 0·75   **d** 0·32   **e** 0·88   **f** 0·05

2 Work out the missing numerators in these fractions.
Check your answers using division.

a

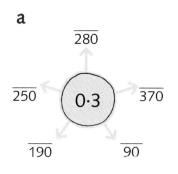

$$\frac{}{280}$$

$$\frac{}{250} \quad 0.3 \quad \frac{}{370}$$

$$\frac{}{190} \qquad \frac{}{90}$$

b

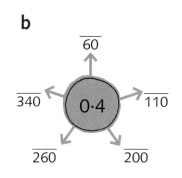

$$\frac{}{60}$$

$$\frac{}{340} \quad 0.4 \quad \frac{}{110}$$

$$\frac{}{260} \qquad \frac{}{200}$$

c

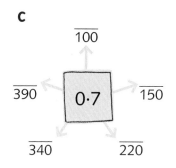

$$\frac{}{100}$$

$$\frac{}{390} \quad 0.7 \quad \frac{}{150}$$

$$\frac{}{340} \qquad \frac{}{220}$$

d

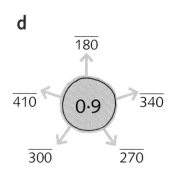

$$\frac{}{180}$$

$$\frac{}{410} \quad 0.9 \quad \frac{}{340}$$

$$\frac{}{300} \qquad \frac{}{270}$$

e

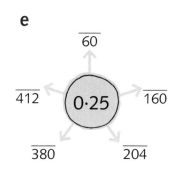

$$\frac{}{60}$$

$$\frac{}{412} \quad 0.25 \quad \frac{}{160}$$

$$\frac{}{380} \qquad \frac{}{204}$$

f

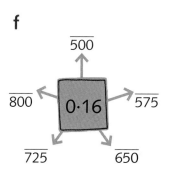

$$\frac{}{500}$$

$$\frac{}{800} \quad 0.16 \quad \frac{}{575}$$

$$\frac{}{725} \qquad \frac{}{650}$$

allenge 3

Play this game with a partner. You will be converting fractions to decimals.

- Take turns to roll both the dice, e.g. 5 and 8.
- Make a fraction with the smaller number as the numerator and the larger number as the denominator, i.e. $\frac{5}{8}$.
- Use division to convert the fraction into a decimal rounded to 2 decimal places, i.e. 0·63.
- Check your answer using a calculator.
- If your answer is correct, this is your score for that round.
- If your answer is incorrect, you score zero.
- After 10 rounds each player adds up their scores.
- The winner is the player with the larger score.

You will need:
- 2 × 0–9 dice
- calculator

Rule:
If you roll a 0, roll the dice again.

Example

$$0 \cdot 6\ 2\ 5$$
$$8\overline{)5\ \cdot^5 0\ ^2 0\ ^4 0}$$

Motorway café pie charts

• Interpret and draw pie charts and use them to solve problems

Challenge 1

Carla carried out a survey of the sales of snacks from the kiosk at the motorway café.
She recorded her results in a percentage pie chart.

1 Write the percentage of customers who chose:

   a crisps   **b** nuts

   c raisins   **d** an apple

2 Write the number of customers who chose:

   a crisps   **b** nuts

   c raisins   **d** an apple

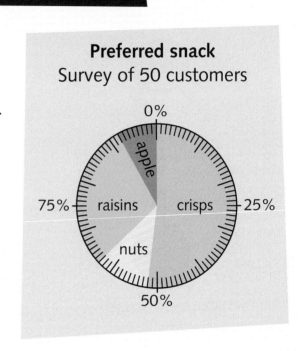

Preferred snack
Survey of 50 customers

Challenge 2

1 The table shows the breakfast orders that Kevin took one morning.

Order	Tally	Frequency	Percentage
Cereal	ⵀⵀⵀ I	6	
Toast and egg	ⵀⵀⵀ ⵀⵀⵀ ⵀⵀⵀ		
Beans and egg	ⵀⵀⵀ ⵀⵀⵀ II		
Full breakfast	ⵀⵀⵀ ⵀⵀⵀ ⵀⵀⵀ III		
	Total		

You will need:
• Resource 52: Pie charts
• ruler
• coloured pencils

• Copy columns 1, 3 and 4 of the table. Complete the frequency column and find the total frequency. Then convert each frequency to a percentage.

• Using Resource 52: Pie charts, draw a percentage pie chart for the breakfast orders. Colour the sectors and make a key for your pie chart.

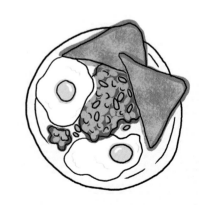

2 The table below shows the type of transport stopping at the café in one day.

- Copy and complete the table. Calculate the total frequency so you can convert each frequency to a percentage.
- Using Resource 52, draw a percentage pie chart for the type of transport using the café. Colour the sectors and make a key for your pie chart.

Transport	Frequency	Percentage
Lorry	54	
Bus	18	
Car	72	
Van	36	
Total		

3 The pie chart shows the sales of 500 hot and cold drinks in one day.

a Write the percentage of sales for:

  i tea   **iii** soft drinks   **v** fresh orange

  ii coffee   **iv** milk

b Write how many customers ordered:

  i tea   **iii** soft drinks   **v** fresh orange

  ii coffee   **iv** milk

c How many more customers ordered hot drinks than cold drinks?

Drinks sales

The café manager gave each adult customer a questionnaire, asking: 'Do you usually order breakfast when you stop at the motorway café?' He collected responses from an equal number of male and female customers.

You will need:
- Resource 52: Pie charts
- ruler
- coloured pencils

a Using Resource 52: Pie charts, draw a percentage pie chart showing the combined male and female responses.

b Write five facts that you can interpret from your pie chart.

Response	Male	Female
Never	12%	14%
Sometimes	16%	26%
Quite often	47%	39%
Very often	18%	16%
Always	7%	5%

Export problems

- Construct and use line graphs to solve problems

Challenge 1

Some of the multiples of the 6 times table are plotted on the grid.

- Copy the four points onto a grid on Resource 73: 9 × 9 coordinate grids.
- Join the points in order as shown.
- Continue to plot the points up to 6 × 12 on the grid then join the points in order.
- Write the coordinates of the points where the pattern repeats.

Example

6 × 1 = 6 is the point (0, 6)
6 × 2 = 12 is the point (1, 2)
6 × 3 = 18 is the point (1, 8)

You will need:
- Resource 73:
  9 × 9 coordinate grids
- ruler

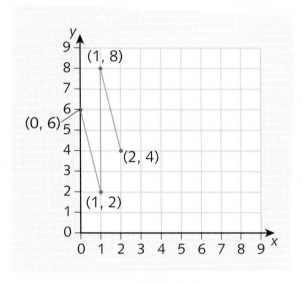

Challenge 2

A British company manufactures and exports golfing goods worldwide. These are the retail prices in the UK for some of their products. Use the information to answer the questions.

You will need:
- Resource 74:
  line graph paper
- ruler

a Take the exchange rate between US dollars and pounds to be £1 = $1.60. Use the table below to plot the points on the graph paper on Resource 74: Line graph paper. Join the points with a straight line.

Sterling (£)	10	20	30	40	50	100
US dollar ($)	16	32	48	64	80	160

b Use your conversion graph to price each golf item, on the page opposite, in dollars. Round the prices to the nearest dollar.

c Use an exchange rate £1 = $1.60 to calculate the total retail cost in dollars ($) of:

i 2 boxes of golf balls

ii a sweater and a cap

iii golf bag and shoes

iv 3 polo shirts

---

allenge 3

1 Take the exchange rate between pounds and euros to be £1 = €1·20.

a Copy and complete the table below.

Sterling (£)	10	20	30	40	50	100
Euro (€)	12					

b Use the table to plot the points on the graph paper on Resource 74: Line graph paper. Join the points with a straight line.

2 The manufacturer gives a 25% discount on the retail price for export orders to Europe. Using the information in Challenge 2, find the total cost in euros (€) of each order.

a 10 golf bags

b 15 golf caps

c 20 pairs of shoes

d 50 boxes of golf balls

e 30 umbrellas

f 60 pairs of gloves

Carrying out a survey

- Collect and organise data to solve problems and plot a graph relating two variables

Challenges 1,2 Work in a small group. Choose one of the questions below to investigate.

Do taller children take a larger shoe size?

Do taller children have a longer arm span?

Do children with a small hand span have small feet?

Can taller children hold their breath for a longer time?

1 Discuss these points in your group:

- what data you will need to collect
- how you will collect the data
- how many children will be included in the survey
- what measuring tools you will need
- what you expect the results to show
- your prediction

You will need:
- measuring tape or metre stick
- ruler
- 1 cm squared paper or graph paper
- seconds timer or stopwatch

2 Everyone in the group should:

- make a frequency table for the data
- record the data in their table.

3 Discuss with your group which type of graph is most suitable for the data. Then draw your graph.

4 Write a statement to compare your results with your prediction in Question 1.

Work with a partner. Investigate the question below.

You will need:
- front page story of a tabloid and a broadsheet newspaper
- 1 cm squared paper
- ruler

How easy are newspapers to read?

1 Decide who will take which newspaper. Begin with the headline. Count and mark off the first 100 words.

2 Copy the frequency table below. This lets you record the number of letters in each word in intervals of four letters. Count the number of letters in each word for the first 100 words in your newspaper, using tally marks to record this data in the table.

Letters per word	Tally	Frequency
1–4		
5–8		
9–12		
13–16		
17 or more		

These count as single words: knock-out, MEP, London's.

3 With your partner, decide on a suitable graph for the data in the table.

- Draw the graph for your newspaper.
- Compare the graphs.
- Write a report about what you have found out.

4 Record the same data again using intervals of three letters.

5 Discuss with your partner which is the more useful set of intervals to use to answer the question. Write the reason for your answer.

Mainly means

- Calculate and interpret the mean as an average of a set of data

Challenge 1

Calculate the mean of each set of numbers and measures.

a 5, 8, 11

b 9, 12, 6

c 2, 7, 7, 8

d 5, 10, 11, 14

e £6, £9, £13, £8

f 10 m, 12 m, 14 m, 16 m

Hint

To find the mean, add the values and divide by the number of values.

Example

4 + 8 + 12 = 24

24 ÷ 3 = 8

Mean = 8

Challenge 2

1 Find the mean of each set of luggage.

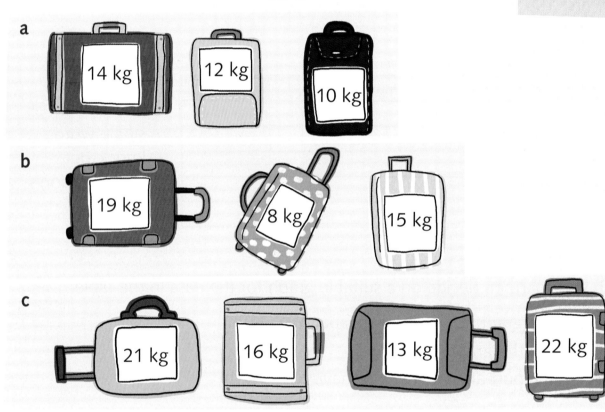

a 14 kg   12 kg   10 kg

b 19 kg   8 kg   15 kg

c 21 kg   16 kg   13 kg   22 kg

2 Calculate in kilograms the mean mass of the five parcels.

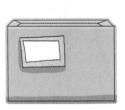  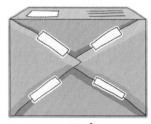 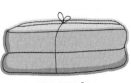

8·62 kg   **9·11 kg**   **8·7 kg**   **11·9 kg**   **8·17 kg**

3 Calculate in litres the mean amount of water in these containers.

3·68 *l* 2·33 *l* 3·5 *l* 2·98 *l* 3·13 *l* 5·86 *l*

4 Last summer the Cole and the Dakin families took their holidays in the same week in July. The Coles went to Kent and the Dakins went to Devon.

a Use the graphs to find the mean number of hours of sunshine per day for each family.

b This table shows the temperature at noon in each place over the week. Use the data in the table to find the mean daily temperature for each holiday.

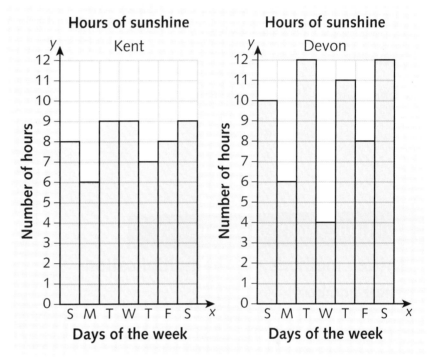

Hours of sunshine — Kent

Hours of sunshine — Devon

Days of the week

Temperature at noon (°C)

	S	M	T	W	T	F	S
Kent	26	24	27	27	26	25	27
Devon	27	24	28	22	27	26	28

Challenge 3

The house numbers in this row of houses increase by two each time. The mean of the house numbers is 18. Find the number of each house.

Maths facts

Addition and subtraction

Whole numbers

Example: 456,287 + 359,849

```
    4 5 6 2 8 7
  + 3 5 9 8 4 9
    8 1 6 1 3 6
    1 1 1 1
```

Example: 746,291 – 298,354

```
  6 13 15 12  8 11        6 13 15  1  8  1
  7  4  6  2  9  1        7  4  6  2  9  1
- 2  9  8  3  5  4      - 2  9  8  3  5  4
  4  4  7  9  3  7        4  4  7  9  3  7
```

> You can also write the exchanged values like this.

Decimals

Example: 57·486 + 45·378

```
    5 7 · 4 8 6
  + 4 5 · 3 7 8
  1 0 2 · 8 6 4
    1     1 1
```

Example: 63·237 – 45·869

```
  5 12   11 12 17       5 12   11 12  1
  6  3 ·  2  3  7       6  3 ·  2  3  7
- 4  5 ·  8  6  9     - 4  5 ·  8  6  9
  1  7 ·  3  6  8       1  7 ·  3  6  8
```

> You can also write the exchanged values like this.

Multiplication and division

Written methods – short multiplication

Whole numbers

Example: 2,654 × 3

Partitioning

$2{,}654 \times 3 = (2{,}000 \times 3) + (600 \times 3) + (50 \times 3) + (4 \times 3)$
$= 6{,}000 + 1{,}800 + 150 + 12$
$= 7{,}962$

Grid method

×	2,000	600	50	4	
3	6,000	1,800	150	12	= 7,962

Expanded written method

```
      2 6 5 4
  ×         3
      1 2      (4 × 3)
    1 5 0      (50 × 3)
  1 8 0 0      (600 × 3)
  6 0 0 0      (2,000 × 3)
  7 9 6 2
```

Formal written method

```
      2 6 5 4          2 6 5 4
  ×         3      ×   1 1 1 3
      7 9 6 2          7 9 6 2
      1 1 1
```

> You can also write the regrouped values like this.

Decimals

Example: 4·83 × 6

Partitioning

$4{\cdot}83 \times 6 = (4 \times 6) + (0{\cdot}8 \times 6) + (0{\cdot}03 \times 6)$
$= 24 + 4{\cdot}8 + 0{\cdot}18$
$= 28{\cdot}98$

Grid method

×	4	0·8	0·03	
6	24	4·8	0·18	= 28·98

Expanded written method

```
       4 · 8 3
  ×          6
       0 · 1 8   (0·03 × 6)
       4 · 8 0   (0·8 × 6)
     2 4 · 0 0   (4 × 6)
     2 8 · 9 8
```

Formal written method

```
       4 · 8 3
  ×          6
     2 8 · 9 8
       4   1
```

We can also work out the answer to this calculation by converting the decimal to a whole number before calculating, then converting the product back to a decimal.
4·83 × 6 is equivalent to 483 × 6 ÷ 100

Written methods – long multiplication

Whole numbers

Example: 285 × 63

Partitioning

$285 \times 63 = (200 \times 63) + (80 \times 63) + (5 \times 63)$
$= 12{,}600 + 5{,}040 + 315$
$= 17{,}955$

Grid method

×	200	80	5
60	12,000	4,800	300
3	600	240	15

    17100
+   855
    17955

Expanded written method

```
        2 8 5
  ×       6 3
          1 5   (5 × 3)
        2 4 0   (80 × 3)
        6 0 0   (200 × 3)
        3 0 0   (5 × 60)
      4 8 0 0   (80 × 60)
    1 2 0 0 0   (200 × 60)
    1 7 9 5 5
        1
```

Formal written method

```
          2 8 5
  ×         6 3
        8² 5¹ 5   (285 × 3)
      1 7⁵ 1³ 0 0   (285 × 60)
      1 7 9 5 5
```

Decimals

Example: 7·56 × 34

Partitioning

$7{\cdot}56 \times 34 = (7 \times 34) + (0{\cdot}5 \times 34) + (0{\cdot}06 \times 34)$
$= 238 + 17 + 2{\cdot}04$
$= 257{\cdot}04$

Grid method

×	7	0·5	0·06
30	210	15	1·8
4	28	2	0·24

   226·80
+   30·24
   257·04

Expanded written method

```
        7 · 5 6
  ×         3 4
        0 · 2 4   (0·06 × 4)
        2 · 0 0   (0·5 × 4)
      2 8 · 0 0   (7 × 4)
        1 · 8 0   (0·06 × 30)
      1 5 · 0 0   (0·5 × 30)
    2 1 0 · 0 0   (7 × 30)
    2 5 7 · 0 4
        1   1
```

Formal written method

```
        7 · 5 6
  ×         3 4
      3 0² · 2² 4   (7·56 × 4)
    2 2¹ 6¹ · 8 0   (7·56 × 30)
    2 5 7 · 0 4
          1
```

We can also work out the answer to this calculation by converting the decimal to a whole number before calculating, then converting the product back to a decimal.

7·56 × 34 is equivalent to 756 × 34 ÷ 100

Written methods – short division
Whole numbers

Example: 1,838 ÷ 8

Expanded written method

```
        2 2 9  r 6
    8)1 8 3 8
    – 1 6 0 0   (200 × 8)
        ¹2 ¹3 8
    –     1 6 0   (20 × 8)
            7 8
    –       7 2   (9 × 8)
              6
```

Formal written method

Whole number remainder

```
      2 2 9 r 6
  8)1 ¹8 ²3 ⁷8
```

Fraction remainder

```
      2 2 9 ³⁄₄
  8)1 ¹8 ²3 ⁷8
```

Decimal remainder

```
      2 2 9 · 7 5
  8)1 ¹8 ²3 ⁷8 ·⁶0 ⁴0
```

Decimals

Example: 45·36 ÷ 6

Regrouping

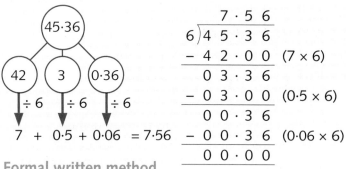

7 + 0·5 + 0·06 = 7·56

Expanded written method

```
        7 · 5 6
    6)4 5 · 3 6
    – 4 2 · 0 0   (7 × 6)
        0 3 · 3 6
    –   0 3 · 0 0   (0·5 × 6)
            0 0 · 3 6
    –       0 0 · 3 6   (0·06 × 6)
                0 0 · 0 0
```

Formal written method

```
      7 · 5 6
  6)4 ⁴5 ·³3 ⁶6
```

We can also work out the answer to this calculation by converting the decimal to a whole number before calculating, then converting the product back to a decimal.

45·36 ÷ 6 is equivalent to 4,536 ÷ 6 ÷ 100

Written methods – long division
Whole numbers

Example: 8,548 ÷ 16

Expanded written method

```
        5 3 4  r 4
    16)8 5 4 8
    – 8 0 0 0   (500 × 16)
        ⁴5 ¹4 8
    –     4 8 0   (30 × 16)
              6 8
    –         6 4   (4 × 16)
                4
```

Formal written method

```
        5 3 4  r 4
    16)8 5 4 8
    –  8 0 ↓
        ⁴5 ¹4 ↓
    –      4 8 ↓
              6 8
    –         6 4
                4
```

8,468 ÷ 16 = 534 r 4 or 534¼ or 534·25

Decimals

Example: 45·64 ÷ 14

Expanded written method

```
        3 · 2 6
    14)4 5 · 6 4
    – 4 2 · 0 0   (3 × 14)
        0 ²3 ·¹6 4
    –   0 2 · 8 0   (0·2 × 14)
            0 0 · 8 4
    –       0 0 · 8 4   (0·06 × 14)
                0 0 · 0 0
```

Formal written method

```
        3 · 2 6
    14)4 5 · 6 4
    –  4 2 · ↓
        ²3 ·¹6 ↓
    –       2 · 8 ↓
              0 · 8 4
    –         0 · 8 4
                0 · 0 0
```

We can also work out the answer to this calculation by converting the decimal to a whole number before calculating, then converting the product back to a decimal.

45·64 ÷ 14 is equivalent to 4,564 ÷ 14 ÷ 100

Fractions, decimals and percentages

$$\frac{1}{100} = 0.01 = 1\%$$

$$\frac{2}{100} = \frac{1}{50} = 0.02 = 2\%$$

$$\frac{4}{100} = \frac{1}{25} = 0.04 = 4\%$$

$$\frac{5}{100} = \frac{1}{20} = 0.05 = 5\%$$

$$\frac{10}{100} = \frac{1}{10} = 0.1 = 10\%$$

$$\frac{20}{100} = \frac{1}{5} = 0.2 = 20\%$$

$$\frac{25}{100} = \frac{1}{4} = 0.25 = 25\%$$

$$\frac{40}{100} = \frac{2}{5} = 0.4 = 40\%$$

$$\frac{50}{100} = \frac{1}{2} = 0.5 = 50\%$$

$$\frac{75}{100} = \frac{3}{4} = 0.75 = 75\%$$

$$\frac{80}{100} = \frac{4}{5} = 0.8 = 80\%$$

$$\frac{100}{100} = \frac{10}{10} = 1 = 100\%$$

Add proper fractions

$$\frac{1}{3} + \frac{2}{5} = \frac{5}{15} + \frac{6}{15}$$
$$= \frac{11}{15}$$

Subtract proper fractions

$$\frac{9}{10} - \frac{2}{3} = \frac{27}{30} - \frac{20}{30}$$
$$= \frac{7}{30}$$

$$\frac{2}{3} \times 4 = \frac{8}{3}$$
$$= 2\frac{2}{3}$$

$$2\frac{3}{4} \times 3 = \frac{11}{4} \times 3$$
$$= \frac{33}{4}$$
$$= 8\frac{1}{4}$$

Add mixed numbers

$$1\frac{2}{3} + 2\frac{3}{4} = 3 + \frac{2}{3} + \frac{3}{4}$$
$$= 3 + \frac{8}{12} + \frac{9}{12}$$
$$= 3\frac{17}{12}$$
$$= 4\frac{5}{12}$$

or

$$1\frac{2}{3} + 2\frac{3}{4} = \frac{5}{3} + \frac{11}{4}$$
$$= \frac{20}{12} + \frac{33}{12}$$
$$= \frac{53}{12}$$
$$= 4\frac{5}{12}$$

Subtract mixed numbers

$$3\frac{1}{5} - 1\frac{2}{3} = 3\frac{3}{15} - 1\frac{10}{15}$$
$$= 2\frac{18}{15} - 1\frac{10}{15}$$
$$= 1\frac{8}{15}$$

or

$$3\frac{1}{5} - 1\frac{2}{3} = \frac{16}{5} - \frac{5}{3}$$
$$= \frac{48}{15} - \frac{25}{15}$$
$$= \frac{23}{15}$$
$$= 1\frac{8}{15}$$

Multiply two proper fractions

$$\frac{3}{4} \times \frac{1}{3} = \frac{3}{12} = \frac{1}{4}$$

Divide a proper fraction by a whole number

$$\frac{2}{3} \div 5 = \frac{2}{3} \times \frac{1}{5} = \frac{2}{15}$$

Measurement

Length

1 km = 1,000 m = 100,000 cm

0·1 km = 100 m = 10,000 cm = 100,000 mm

0·01 km = 10 m = 1,000 cm = 10,000 mm

1 m = 100 cm = 1,000 mm

0·1 m = 10 cm = 100 mm

0·01 m = 1 cm = 10 mm

0·001 m = 0·1 cm = 1 mm

1 cm = 10 mm

0·1 cm = 1 mm

Metric units and imperial units – Length

1 km $\approx \frac{5}{8}$ miles (8 km $\approx$ 5 miles)

1 inch $\approx$ 2·5 cm

Perimeter, area and volume

P = perimeter   A = area   V = volume

l = length w = width b = base h = height

Perimeter of a rectangle
$P = 2(l + w)$

Perimeter of a square
$P = 4 \times l$ or $P = 4l$

Area of a rectangle
$A = l \times w$ or $A = lw$

Area of a triangle
$A = \frac{1}{2} \times b \times h$ or $A = \frac{1}{2}bh$

Area of a parallelogram
$A = b \times h$ or $A = bh$

Volume of a cuboid
$V = l \times w \times h$ or $V = lwh$

Capacity

1 litre = 1,000 ml

0·1 l = 100 ml

0·01 l = 10 ml

0·001 l = 1 ml

1 cl = 10 ml

24-hour time

Mass

1 t = 1,000 kg   1 kg = 1,000 g   0·1 kg = 100g   0·01 kg = 10 g   0·001 kg = 1 g

Geometry

Parts of a circle

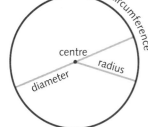

Coordinates

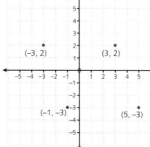

Translation

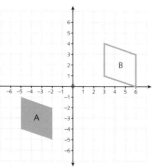

Shape A has been translated 8 squares to the right and 5 squares up.

Reflection

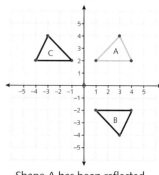

Shape A has been reflected in the x-axis (Shape B) and in the y-axis (Shape C).